Mary Ellen Kerr
Psalm 34:7

watched

MARY ELLEN KERR

Copyright © 2011 by Mary Ellen Kerr
First Edition – December 2011

ISBN
978-1-77097-003-8 (Hardcover)
978-1-77097-004-5 (Paperback)
978-1-77097-005-2 (eBook)

All rights reserved.

No part of this publication may be reproduced in any form, or by any means, electronic or mechanical, including photocopying, recording, or any information browsing, storage, or retrieval system, without permission in writing from the publisher.

This book is a work of fiction. Names, characters, places, and incidents either are products of the author's imagination or are used fictitiously. Any resemblance to actual events or locales or persons, living or dead, is entirely coincidental.

Published by:

FriesenPress
Suite 300 – 852 Fort Street
Victoria, BC, Canada V8W 1H8

www.friesenpress.com

Distributed to the trade by The Ingram Book Company

Chapter 1

Joshua was born under extremely stressful times. His mother Yolanda had been living in the worst part of town. She had been trying to get her family to better circumstances for years. The projects however, are unrelenting and life was hard. Money was in short supply so Yolanda decided to have Joshua at home instead of a clean hospital room foregoing the help that would be there at a moment's notice. It was three a.m. and no one was home. The other children had been taken from her a few days earlier and placed in foster care because of a domestic disturbance by an abusive husband. Being so far along in her pregnancy, Yolanda couldn't get to the Social Service Office to make arrangements to bring the three other children back home and thought perhaps they were better there until she could have this baby. She could only focus on one thing these days and that was getting this baby born and being done with it.

"So this is when you are going to enter this world. It's just like you to come into my life, when no one is around and your brothers and sisters are almost grown." she said while rubbing her stomach and feeling time was short. Jeremiah was seventeen, Trinity was sixteen, and Elisha was fifteen, and now she was having this child just when she thought she would get her life and her children to a better place, away from the projects. She spoke to this new life that she had decided months earlier to name Joshua. He was about to emerge into this world of turmoil and hardship. Labor had been easy at first, but now, she was alone, and scared. She sensed something was terribly wrong but didn't know how to assess what it was. 'I have to do this' she thought. 'There is just no other way.'

Joshua was coming with more complications than Yolanda had expected. After laboring for two hours, Yolanda decided she needed to call her friend Trish. Trish would come at a moment's notice if she were home. Trish was an attractive girl with a full figure and a friendly personality and she had a tendency to sleep around, some nights never making it back to her residence. As she dialed the number, pain began to come in shorter intervals.

When Trish answered the phone, she heard Yolanda say, "Something is terribly wrong. Trish, I need you right now. The baby is coming and I don't think I can do this alone."

Trish had been home alone studying, she had fallen asleep in the chair with a book in her lap. She had made the decision months earlier to better her life and stop carousing. She was a waitress at a local club, but with the decision to improve her life, wasn't working as much so she could take classes at the local community college and have time to study.

When Trish heard Yolanda on the phone she knew immediately something was wrong. "I'll be right there, you just hang on. Do you want me to call for help?"

"No, I just need you to come," she replied in a painful whisper.

Trish hung up the phone, grabbed her keys, and ran to the car. She could be at Yolanda's in ten minutes if she sped and there wasn't any traffic. Who would be on the streets at three a.m. she thought. Just as she turned the corner for Yolanda's house, she saw a group of young men hanging out on the street.

'Oh great' she thought, 'just what I need a gang of thugs hanging out in the hood.' As she approached the young men, she realized one of them was Yolanda's oldest son, Jeremiah.

"It's ironic how Yolanda named those boys after good men in the Bible and how they have turned to a life of crime," she said out loud.

She slowed the car to a stop; just as one of the men approached her asking if she wanted to buy something to make her life sweeter. She brushed him off and hollered to Jeremiah. "Get yourself over here Jeremiah. Your mama's having a baby and she needs help."

"Who you talken to ho?" Jeremiahs voice sounded a bit slurred and certainly not sober.

"Jeremiah your mama is having her baby and she is having trouble. You be respectful. Come and help!"

"What can I do? I don't know notten about delivering babies. I only knows how to make em." This made the guys with him laugh. He knew this was just to show off in front of the brothers but he felt a bit ashamed he had called Trish a ho; she was one of his mother's best friends.

"Well get out of my way! She is needen me and I need to get over there. Whatcha doing out here anyway? I thought that social service lady came and got you, your sister and brother and took you all to the group home?"

"Yeah she did, but they can't keep me. I snuck out and got away when everyone was asleep. I isn't staying at that stinking hole. They didn't even know I was leaven and wouldn't have dared stop me if they did," he said.

"Well you best be at your mama's home quick like to see how she and the baby is doing." Trish shut the window and started on her way.

"Yeah, yeah, I'll stop by." Was Jeremiahs response, and off they went into the night 'to do who knows what,' Trish thought.

In the heavenly realm angelic beings were watching the events of the Lance family and waiting to be dispatched by the mere sound of a prayer entering the heavenly portal.

At that precise moment, Yolanda in tears and pain, dropped to her knees and asked God to help her through what she knew would be more than she could do on her own.

"Oh Jesus, I need your help more now than I have ever needed it. I just know something is terribly wrong, and I can't do this on my own. Please send help and help this baby to be born healthy. Give him a better life."

The contractions came again, and she couldn't finish her prayer. Just at that moment, angels were dispatched with such speed that no human could understand or perceive. The watchers had been awaiting a signal from the prayer room. Timon, an angel with coffee and cream colored features, dark eyes and powerful wings, sped to Trish's location and began to guide her through the streets to make sure there wasn't anything that would delay her arrival to Yolanda's house. Rafael, the other watcher and commander of a mighty legion headed for Yolanda's house. Rafael was handsome. He had mocha colored skin, long golden hair tied in the back and crystal blue eyes, and a wing span of over seven feet. They knew this would be a night of human pain and suffering and yet a night of joy only the heavens could understand.

Yolanda was losing the battle, and the baby was struggling to move through the door of life when Trish came crashing into the house.

"Yolanda where are you?" she screamed as she rushed from room to room.

As she approached the bedroom, she found Yolanda lying on the floor. Blood was all around her, and she had the look of death on her face. Trish screamed for help but no one was there or at least she didn't see anyone. At that moment two very strong men came to the rescue and helped her place Yolanda on the bed. They instructed her to call 911 and tell them to hurry. When Trish looked around the two men were no longer there, and she thought she must surely be losing her mind. She dialed 911 and told the operator that her friend was in trouble, the baby was coming, and Yolanda was not breathing. The operator instructed her to begin CPR, but Trish had never done anything like that and panicked at the thought of it. She might hurt the baby, and she didn't want to be responsible for killing or hurting the baby. As she was arguing with the dispatcher about administering CPR, she heard a noise at the front door. The operator said, "It must be the paramedics, go let them in." As she raced to the door, Jeremiah came crashing in. "What's the matter Trish? Where's mama?"

"Oh Jeremiah, something's terribly wrong. She isn't breathing, and I think the baby is coming. I don't know what to do!" she yelled hysterically.

Jeremiah raced to the bedroom only to find his mother turning blue; there was blood all over the floor. As the adrenalin of the situation began to kick in, so did the panic and he was instantly sober.

He began to cry, "Mama, Mama, wake up, please wake up, don't leave me, we all need you." as he held her hand.

The paramedics burst through the front door and came directly to the bedroom: They seemed to know exactly where to go and what to do. They had been directed and guided the entire way by two heavenly beings and were never aware of the help.

Pandemonium had struck the little house on Mello Street. The paramedics worked frantically to save Yolanda's life as well as the baby. Trish was in the living room moaning and crying "Lorda mighty help them men save Yolanda and that baby." Jeremiah was in the kitchen, sobbing uncontrollably, bargaining with God, "I need my mamma." He promised to be a better son and go to church. "God don't let her die." The alcohol and drugs were again affecting his emotions, and he was having a hard time controlling his thoughts, let alone his actions. He sank to the floor and began sobbing. That night Joshua came through the door of life. He entered into a world that would lead to a battle for his very soul. Yolanda entered through the door that led to peace eternal. She entered the heavenly realm by her faith in the only man she had ever really trusted, Jesus Christ.

Timon was the angel appointed to Yolanda's case. His name meant honorable, deemed worthy and he waited patiently for Yolanda to enter through the door and lead her home. Rafael remained to watch over the newest being. Rafael was given command to guide this new life to the place that one day his faith would allow access through the door to peace.

Chapter 2

Social Services would take custody of Joshua Lance upon his discharge from the hospital. His mother had died during childbirth. The funeral was held in a small Baptist Church that Yolanda had attended off and on most of her life. Her husband disappeared to who knew where. He had heard about Yolanda and was sorry, but he wasn't about to take on the responsibility of four kids. Kids always cramped his style of gambling and carousing. Her children had been in attendance at the funeral only to find that they would be taken in separate directions at the end of the service. Social Services could not place four children together, especially since three were teenagers and one a new born. Jeremiah left that day bitter and resentful. He was especially mad at God for not listening to his prayer to allow his mother to live. In a few months he would be old enough to join the armed service and get out of this place that held so many painful memories. He would use his anger to fight a physical enemy, but his soul was fighting a battle against all the injustices he felt in his life and the life of those in the projects and, against God Almighty. Elisha was in a state of shock. He had been his mother's pet child, always obedient and helpful when needed. The Social Service lady said she had a family that wanted to take him and that he would be well cared for. With much reluctance he said he would go. However the new family was abusive, and Elisha ran away, back to the gang he had been initiated into when he was thirteen. Elisha eventually ended up going to prison for beating another gang member so severely, he almost died; Elisha was given ten years in prison after serving three years in juvenile detention. Trinity, the middle child, was always fighting for her place in the family. She had made a decision early on in high school that she would not live the same lifestyle her mother had. She was going to escape the projects and never return. She was allowed to move in with Trish who said she would clean up her act and be a mother to Trinity the best she could. Trinity threw herself into studies at school and became valedictorian of her class and then went on to attend college. Trish and Trinity would often study together as they both had a vision of their life being better. These choices would give them both a better life than their parents had been given. Trinity eventually became a social worker and vowed to help others who had found themselves in the situation her family had been in. Trish eventually found herself in a relationship with someone she had met at college. They married after Trish found herself pregnant.

That left Joshua, the baby, whom his mother had asked God to watch over. He was going to be adopted by a white, upper middle class family and raised with so much more than his mother could have ever expected to be possible. Was this the life Yolanda had wanted for her child? Only time would tell.

Joshua's attending angel, Rafael, commander of legions was watching from his vantage point in the heavens. The fallen, those angels who had left there place in heaven, were also watching and would be waiting for an opportunity to create discord and havoc in Joshua's life. The fallen were a patient lot and would come upon a life in the least expected moment. They could wait. It was only a matter of time until sin would give them an advantage, and then they would pounce on those un-expecting victims.

Chapter 3

Joshua's first years of life were a struggle; the trauma from the birth must have affected this young soul as he was fussy and easily agitated. The Hardgrave family was patient and loving but found this young black child to be a handful with late night crying and what seemed to be fits of anger. Nancy Hardgrave was an emergency room nurse at the local hospital. She was average height, with square shoulders and a solid built. She had brown hair, that she wore pulled back into a pony tail and her round face always had a smile. Nancy had been in attendance to check out Joshua when the Emergency Management Team brought him in for observation. She had immediately made a connection with this young life and when the Social Services case worker came, she gave their names to be placed on a list to adopt Joshua if he ever became available. William Hardgrave, a tall, lean man with a thick head of curly hair and a pleasing personality was employed by a law firm that specialized in family financial planning. They had desired a child of their own since they married ten years earlier but the doctor said Nancy wasn't able to conceive and that adoption was their only choice to ever having a family of their own. The Hardgrave's attended a local Presbyterian Church and were upstanding members of the community. The day came that Social Services contacted them that Joshua Lance would be available for adoption. The Hardgrave's had gone through all the applications and paperwork and were informed the adoption would be final within a month. They would become the parents of Joshua. They finalized the adoption by changing Joshua's last name to Hardgrave. The birth mother had left a letter stating this child should be called Joshua in the event anything happened to her, so the Hardgrave's decided to honor that request. They seemed the ideal family with one exception, their son would be of another race and they lived in the south. The adoption became final within his first month after birth.

Chapter 4

"I believe it would be to Joshua's advantage if he attended a private school, perhaps we could enroll him in the Somerset Academy." Somerset was a school started in nine-teen fifty five by a group of leading citizens. These leaders in the community wanted to have their children receive a superior education, in a segregated atmosphere. Over the years, growth in the community with a more liberal board, rules were relaxed. However, Somerset Academy remained segregated. The high tuition seemed to keep minorities from attending. "What do you think of that William?" asked Nancy on Joshua's fifth birthday.

"Do you think they would even consider accepting him given he is African American?" said William. "Somerset Academy has been in the area for a long time with roots dating pretty far back. Do you think it wise to submit Joshua to that kind of scrutiny from people that have deep engrained ideas?"

"I have spoken with some of the board members and they think having a black boy attend their school would be good for everyone. It will show that they are more open and more politically correct, sort of speak to today's atmosphere in the world."

"I know their academics are really good and they have a football team that could use some help, and well, it is rather prestigious to come from there. If they will accept him, I think it would be a good fit. We can always remove him if we see he is having problems." William wasn't convinced this was the best decision, but Nancy was sure it would give Joshua a good education and introduce him to some important people.

The decision was made for Joshua to attend the all-white private school called Somerset at the young age of six.

When Joshua entered school he began to see people were different. He had seen this in church where he was the only boy of color, and friends that came to visit were all white. In his life, color was never an issue; his mother had explained that he was special and that was why his skin was darker. That had been a good enough explanation for a child. The other children in his class didn't seem to understand that explanation, however, and he felt they just considered him to be less than they were. He didn't look like the other children, and they didn't look like him. This would be the beginning of his life struggle to find his place.

In the heavens the watchers were keeping an eye on this young soul. The fallen as well as the righteous were watching. The fallen were always planning and scheming, trying to turn Joshua's attention to the fact that others disliked him and made him feel alone. God's protecting angels were always waiting for the time to rescue and protect.

Chapter 5

Joshua had made it through his primary and elementary years without a lot of stress. He was a bright child and learned his lessons quickly. Children without the prompting of adults seem to get along. They don't seem to mistrust unless they were taught to mistrust. So Joshua made friends at school although he was never invited to anyone's home to play. He did make friends with a girl named Patricia Forrester and he called her Patty. She would make her way to his home as often as she could and they would play and talk and became close friends. Their friendship continued on to their senior year in high school.

In Joshua's teens he developed body changes as well as the emotions that go along with a young boy's growth. These emotions hit at the same time he began to consider who his family of origin was. He had thought of his birth-family; the one that probably looked more like him than the parents that had been raising him. He had thought of them many times over the years, but it seemed more important to him now since he would be going off to college and he would be on his own.

Joshua had become a handsome, soon to be man with smooth chocolate skin, dark eyes that seemed to dance when he watched you and a mischievous smile that would break out at a moment's notice showing his perfectly aligned white teeth. His hair was cropped short due more to his white up-bringing than his heritage, and he had strong square shoulders. During his high school years he had attained a weight of one hundred and seventy five pounds and a six foot one frame that made his presence known when he entered a room. In another setting than Somerset, he would have had girls forever chasing after him.

Without his parents being aware, Joshua had begun a search. A "Plan of Discovery" he called it, and before heading off to college he was determined to discover who he was and where his family of origin was.

In the realm where the fallen watchers waited, cheers of sheer delight broke out. They soon would be ready to intervene on his life; they knew orders would be given soon to move.

"Soon we will be able to start work," one of the more evil, fallen watchers spoke with a snort. "We have been a long time waiting for this day to arrive. We must inform the ranks and begin to intervene in his decisions, make tempting situations that will be hard for him to turn away from." The evil's contorted expression would have made chills up the spine if seen in the human arena.

"He soon will be ours," declared the imp-like figure of an evil-one as they descended into what looked like a man hole in the earth.

Chapter 6

"I'll begin with the internet to see if I can find any relatives," he said to himself. Joshua knew that there were brothers and sisters in his family, he had overheard conversations his parents had when they didn't know he was listening. He knew one day he would go back to his place of birth and find the answers to questions that were haunting him. In the meantime he would continue to have relationships at school, do his work, play football, and be the good boy everyone expected him to be. On the inside he wanted to break free, to go wild and taste life to the fullest, or at least the life he thought would be the fullest.

"Joshua what are you thinking about? You're so deep in thought you haven't heard a word I have been saying," said Patricia a petite blonde with a great figure and easy smile. Patty had developed into a real beauty and was the only person he could feel really comfortable with. Patricia's family wasn't delighted that they were such close friends but allowed it as long as they were with others, not alone, and always in the public eye. Her parents didn't know that she would go to his house almost every day after school when they were in grade school. She said she was going to the park and she would head to his house. So over the years it was only natural they were the best of friends.

"I'm thinking about going to the dance with you," he said with that little crooked smile that made her want to jump into his arms.

"Well, this is the first I've heard of it. I didn't even know you wanted to go to the dance." She said hoping against all hope that he would want to take her. Given the situation at home she didn't know how she was going to pull this off even though she was sure she was going to figure it out. There wasn't anything she wanted more than to be with Joshua, have him hold her, kiss her and maybe even more. She was also of the age where she dreamed of romance and passion and who better to have that with than this hunk of a handsome guy that everyone noticed when he walked by.

"Well I have been, and I couldn't think of anyone I would rather go with. Are you up to the challenge?" he asked.

"Challenge, whatever are you talking about, a challenge?" She knew she was going to have problems with her family but she didn't think he was talking about her personal challenge.

"I'm talking about all the people who are going to be whispering and snickering at us being together as a date. You know, holding hands, dancing, are you up for that challenge?" He was sure she was, but he didn't want her to not be prepared for the events that could happen.

"That is not a challenge Mr. Hardgrave. That would be my honor. You know me; I love a good challenge. Anyway, remember when that kid in the sixth grade came to school dressed like a homeless kid? Everyone made fun of him. I sat with him at lunch and told him not to worry about what those other kids said. If he wanted, I would show him around and even show him where he could get some cool clothes, and I would help him fit in? I didn't care what those other small-minded people thought. He eventually moved away, but while he was here, he at least didn't get picked on as much as he could have."

Somewhere in his deeper self this made him a little uneasy. Was he just another project of Patricia's, someone that needed fixing, and she was going to show everyone she could fix him?

"Yeah I remember that kid was grateful that the likes of a pretty blonde girl would take such an interest in him. Didn't he end up falling in love with you or something?" he asked.

"Well I guess you could call it love. It was in the sixth grade, and I don't think love is the right word, maybe gratitude. Anyway it made his life easier, and the challenge as you call it wasn't as big a deal as some would think." she turned to leave.

"What time do you want to pick me up or do you want me to meet you at the dance?" she asked.

This surprised Joshua. Meet you at the dance must mean she didn't want him coming to her house as that might be more of a challenge than she had anticipated on the home front. "I'll let you know, gotta see if I can get transportation, and if this is a yes, you will go with me, then I will have to see about purchasing tickets. Would you rather I didn't come to your house?" he asked off-handed.

Patricia hadn't thought this through yet. She would have to broach the issue with her parents and she was giving herself some lee-way in case they said no, she wasn't allowed to have an actual date with a black boy. She had decided already it didn't make any difference what they said; she was going one way or another.

"No, that isn't it," she lied. "I just have to ask my parents if I can go. We will talk again. I'm excited about going." With that, she waved good-bye and headed for her home. She would have to figure out just how she was going to convince her parents to get their permission to go on a date to the prom, no less with Joshua Hardgrave.

Joshua was exhilarated. This would be his first date, his first dance, and his first interracial experience with the public's eye on him. His family had been over-protective in this area and had discouraged him from interracial, co-ed school functions that would make him a target for confrontation. He was a senior now and had decided they couldn't control his decisions any longer. He was becoming an adult. He was constantly in a struggle being a black boy in a white home, a white school and a white society. These feelings only made him want to find out more about his own personal family, his own color, and his own identity. There must be a story and he was more determined than ever to find the truth. He had vowed this night was going to be the beginning of his moving closer to his true identity, and it would all begin with his trip to visit a man he had found on the internet.

Chapter 7

Patricia waited until after dinner when her father would be more receptive to her suggestion to go to the dance with Joshua Hardgrave.

"Daddy," Patricia started with a smile, "I've been invited to the dance. It's okay if I go, right." She posed the question as a statement and waited for the barrage of questions that would follow.

"Well, I wouldn't expect any less from my young princess." He smiled proudly at his daughter. "Just who is the lucky young man?"

"It's Joshua Hardgrave, you know William Hardgrave the lawyer's son," she said still smiling.

A dark shadow came over her father's face as he glanced at his wife who seemed shocked that her daughter would even broach a subject like this with her father.

"Absolutely not young lady! You know how this family stands on this issue. The Hardgrave's are good people, and I believe they think they have done an honorable thing taking a young, helpless black boy into their home. But when it comes to inter-racial mixing, it just isn't the right thing and it certainly isn't going to be perpetuated by anyone in this family. Do I have to remind you that this young man is of another race, a different color and we do not mix those colors in this house?" he said leaving the table with a start. "I'll hear no more of this kind of talk. I have told you before that you can be friends. I was afraid this might happen, but friends at a distance are all that it can be. End of discussion!" as he stormed out of the room.

"But daddy!" She tried to get out before her father left the room. She wanted to be able to give her opinion of what he had said and give her side of the argument.

"No buts about it, young lady. I am aware you like to rescue things; birds, kittens, even a squirrel one time, but you are not going to rescue the Hardgrave's black boy."

Patricia's father forbidding the date made her eventually tell him she would go with some girls and they would be meeting at the school. She hated lying to her parents, but she wasn't going to allow them to stop her from the one night she had been dreaming of for months. She wasn't going to hurt Joshua's feeling, and she wasn't going to consider going with anyone else even though she hadn't been asked by anyone else.

She called to tell Joshua. "Josh, my parents are having a party with a lot of people coming the night of the dance, and it would be best to just meet at the school. I hope you don't mind, but it would just be easier, okay?" Another lie she thought but all for a good reason.

"Sure no problem, I'll see you at the entrance and I'll recognize you how?" he said teasing her.

"Well I'll be the blonde wearing a blue dress and a smile. I'll be looking for the handsomest guy entering the dance," she said and laughed.

That made him smile. He knew she was lying about her parents having a party but decided this would be best. He wouldn't have to deal with her parents who he knew didn't want her seeing him. He could feel that prejudice coming from them the first time they met. He would meet her at the school in the front lobby and he knew she would be beautiful.

The Hardgrave's on the other hand were delighted that Joshua was going to the dance and offered to help him with anything he might need. He had received his license a month earlier and would be allowed to use the family car. There was to be no drinking and he was to be home by midnight. He purchased the tickets and rented a tuxedo. He even bought Patricia a corsage even though it felt a little hokey to do so. He had been thinking of this night ever since the fliers went up about the dance, and he had run every scenario over in his mind from the snickers to an all-out fight, or possibly more enjoyably, an intimate encounter with Patricia. He was ready, and he was even looking forward to the challenge. When he was in the city he must remember to stop at a drug store and buy some condoms. He wanted to be totally prepared for every possible event of the night.

In the recesses of darkness where the fallen ones gathered, there was a furious debate going on as to how this night would play out. Possibly with drinking, fights, sexual encounters, perhaps even death. They snickered and sneered and evil laughter erupted as they plotted how this night would be the night that changed the course of this young man's future, and they would gain control of his very soul.

The watchers of righteousness waited and observed as well. Since the watchers of righteousness had not been enlisted with prayer yet, they had to wait for the command to rescue and protect. They were bound by the law of prayer, and they could not move off their post until enlisted to do so. The righteous watchers were ever vigilant to the Father's commands and would never disobey even when they could see their charges in grave danger. It was their commander who gave the orders and they knew he was always mindful and always watchful to the timing of events. So they watched, and they waited and even turned their eyes aside when their charges did grave and sinful acts. They knew the pain of sin. It had affected the heavenly realm at one time, and the Father had cast the leader of rebellion out of heaven. When he left, he took with him a large number of followers, and they were now considered the fallen. They roamed the earth following their leader's orders to wreak havoc and mayhem on the unsuspecting ones that the Father had marked for great destinies. This night would be a night the righteous watchers would observe with pain just knowing the fallen had plans to try and turn a young man's soul toward evil schemes.

Chapter 8

Joshua had made all the preparations for the dance, but there was one more thing he wanted to do before he felt he was ready for this big event. On the internet he had met a man, someone he thought would be the one to help, one in which he could confide in and tell how he really felt or at least that is what he was hoping for.

Thomas Johnson was a sixty seven year old black man; however he could have been older by the weathered look of his face. His five foot six frame had seen some hard times by the way he was bent at the waist. He had strong biceps and walked with a slight limp. He had dark chocolate colored skin and was balding. He wore jeans and a T-shirt that said 'Keep the Faith'. He came from the wrong side of the tracks, and it was home to him. He had been raised in a family of twelve, with a father who would come and go from job to job. His mother was a strong influence, as was his grandmother. They were very religious and made a profound impact on his life, although it was many years later and several years into incarceration when he made any personal commitments to faith himself. He had been involved in activities that had caused pain to his family, and he had done things that, looking back on, made him feel shame. He made a commitment to the Lord while in prison and now was trying the best he could to live a life that was pleasing to Him. He had created a web site that spoke to young black men about the issues of life that seemed to always lead them in the wrong direction; drugs, alcohol, sex, dropping out of school. He was always trying to encourage boys and young black men to do good instead of running and ripping in the streets. He had published articles on the web about strong black men and their struggles to find true identity. These were the issues that caught Joshua's attention and had made him contact Thomas Johnson.

Joshua had called Mr. Johnson a few days earlier, and Johnson agreed to meet him at a local restaurant in the city. Joshua would skip school on Friday to make the trip. His father allowed him to take the car for school for a "project" that needed him to stay late. He hated lying to his father, but this had become such an obsession that he justified it as a bigger commitment to knowledge of the truth.

Chapter 9

Joshua felt out of his element when he drove into the inner city to meet Mr. Thomas Johnson, but he told himself, he would be fine and actually realized he didn't look as out of place here as he did in school, color-wise anyway.

When he reached the meeting location, he was sure he would be able to pick Mr. Johnson out of a crowd; however he found there were many older black men in the restaurant. Anyone of them could be who he was looking for. He hadn't been to this part of the city before. His parents told him that it could be trouble, and they didn't want him to go anywhere near the likes of it. He didn't find it so offensive and found his way easily. When Joshua entered the restaurant, Mr. Johnson got up from his booth and went to meet him. Joshua noticed his height, his balding head and his large biceps. Thomas Johnson was wearing a large smile that shined with gold on all of his top teeth, and he walked with a limp.

Thomas Johnson could easily see this young black boy didn't fit in here. His clothes were more of a classic white boys dress. No slouchy pants; Joshua's were at an acceptable distance to his waist with a belt that held them up. He wore an Abercrombie & Fitch T-shirt. Most black men wouldn't be caught dead in an uppity white shirt like that, and khaki pants were hardly ever seen in this part of town.

Joshua was a little taken aback by this black man coming towards him with a hand held out and a booming voice of hello. However, he made Joshua feel completely at ease within seconds.

"Well my young friend, what is it you have come to discover today, perhaps a black man's dreams of escape or what it is truly like to be a black man in the world today?" He had a grin on his face and Joshua kept looking at those shinny teeth that totally put him off-base.

"No sir, I am not sure why I am here except I have had a deep sense of loss for so long. I need to find someone to help me escape from that nagging feeling that I belong someplace else other than where I am at present." He was rather sheepish as he said this. It was the first time he had verbally said those words and when they escaped his lips he wasn't sure he wanted them out there for someone else to hear.

"Well my boy, maybe we can find some kind of answers to your dilemma, but first let's have something to eat. Are you hungry?" Thomas Johnson knew that food and drink would be a good distracter to make this young man a little more relaxed. He could tell Joshua was a little uncomfortable with his surroundings. Joshua wasn't aware that this man had done some praying before the meeting, and Thomas Johnson believed God had orchestrated their time together.

In the dark recesses of the fallen arena was screeching at the very idea someone was praying for their victim. The evil watchers had seen Joshua as a clear target, someone that would be easily influenced in the next few days. This was making their job more troublesome than they had anticipated. At the same time, Rafael had begun to stir his comrades to battle. He had been awaiting the day of command when he could go to his charge with full authority from his commander.

"Step aside evil one. Today is my day, and you have no place here. Go back to the hole you came from." Rafael was on the scene before the fallen noticed his arrival. His wings were spread to the fullest, and his face was shining as he descended from his heavenly outpost.

As the fallen watchers escaped through time and space back to their evil chambers, one screeched he would return and be victorious, just wait and see.

Joshua's angel, Rafael, had set up a perimeter around the restaurant. He wanted to make sure his charge had every opportunity to hear what Mr. Johnson wanted to share with him, and he hoped he would accept the truth. These decisions were always in the human's hands as they had been given the opportunity by God to choose for themselves what or who they would follow.

"Choose this day who you will service young charge. May it be the choice for Truth," Rafael said as he watched and waited.

Chapter 10

After eating and making small talk about the drive in and the weather and school, Mr. Johnson got down to the business at hand. "Okay young man what is it that this wise old man can tell you today that will help you on your path to success?" he said with a big shiny, smile.

"Well Mr. Johnson I just don't feel like I fit in anywhere. I am told my mother died when I was born, and I was given to a white family to be raised. They have been good to me and I have a pretty decent life but it just seems like something is missing. My parents, or the people who raised me, don't want to tell me much about my family, and I can't understand why. I know I have brothers and sisters; I've overheard my parents discussing it, but they are very hushed about it and won't say anything to me. I need to know where I fit into this world other than where I am today." As he said this, he began to relax, he had never told anyone about his life and never let anyone close enough to ask any questions other than the fact that he had been adopted and was thankful, he guessed, for what he had. Patricia had prodded him from time to time, but he would only tell her that he didn't know and would she please leave it alone. He really liked her, but she was too much of a rescuer and he didn't want to be rescued. He wanted to know the truth.

Mr. Johnson listened, a skill he had learned long ago. If someone was going to trust you, they had to know you were hearing them and that you cared about what they were saying.

"Let me get this straight, Joshua," Mr. Johnson said. "You feel living this good life, in a nice house, in a good school with decent parents, that you don't feel you fit there, am I right?" he asked.

Joshua began to feel a little defensive, maybe this wasn't a good idea after all, he thought.

"Well, yeah, sorta like that, I mean, I'm black in a white world." he said.

"Well the way I see it my young friend, God has had His hand on you for a long time, keeping you safe and protected. You just haven't realized who it is that is doing the protecting. Now maybe He is prodding you to go a little deeper into your life and find your family." He didn't know if this young man had any spirituality but he was sure going to try and show him God was watching over the situation.

"Well yeah, I guess you could be right. I go to church with my parents, and they talk about being a good person and doing the right things. I try to do that, but I don't see where God has much of a part in the other parts of my life." He was being truthful in his statement; he didn't see how God had much to do with him finding his family. He hadn't helped him yet.

"Well son, I think God has a bigger part in your life than you think. Do you know that your name Joshua means Jehovah is salvation? I think He wants you to understand He is a big God, and He has brought you to this day where you can come to know Him in a personal way." Thomas said a prayer under his breath, "Lord let this young man see the truth and accept you today."

"I didn't' know my name meant that, and that is nice'n all, but what does that have to do with finding out who I am and where my family is?" He was trying to be respectful but was beginning to feel he was getting a lesson on religion and that wasn't what he had come for.

"Well you see son, as soon as a soul comes into this world God has him marked to be saved, Jehovah is salvation. He has been waiting for the right time for you to come to know the truth and the truth will set you free. This could be that time." He was hoping Joshua was getting what he was telling him.

"Are you aware of how many young black men coming from this part of town end up dead? They don't take their education serious, they see easy money selling drugs and getting caught up in gangs, then they go to prison and get meaner and madder or they get killed in the hood. God has kept you from that type of life. He's seen to it that you got an education and kept you from gang activity. He definitely has been watching over you for something special. God wants you to make a decision to use all this life for His work." he said. "Would you like to make a decision for His service?" Thomas asked, hoping he hadn't come on to fast and too strong.

"That is all nice for you Mr. Johnson but I'm not looking to get religion. I'm looking for my family and maybe this has been a mistake coming today. You seem to be some kind of preacher, and I guess I'm looking for some kind of private investigator." He was trying to figure out how he could end this conversation and be on his way.

"Now hold on son, you got me all wrong. I guess I do sound like a preacher. I had lots of time to learn about who I'm talken about when I was in prison, and I saw how God helped a lot a young fella's outa their problems. I'm just saying maybe you oughta give Him a try." Thomas relaxed and decided it was up to God to bring this young man to a decision. He saw he couldn't keep Joshua and thought he should have taken more time, asked more questions and not been so eager to get him to make a decision on the spot.

"Can I tell you one story before you leave?" he asked.

Joshua thought it wouldn't hurt to hear his story, and it might be interesting.

"Sure go ahead I still have some time." he said.

"While I was in prison a young man came in from Juvenile Detention to do a ten year stretch for nearly killing another gang banger. He came in angry and full of hate. He ended up being my bunkie and he wanted me to think he was a tough guy. God had already shown me he was hurting and scared. You see, he only acted that way because he didn't want anybody to see who he really was. I took him under my wing and got him to go to Chapel, got him to begin to read the Bible and we started doing a study to find out why he was so angry. His mother had died during child birth. He had a father who was never around, and when he was he, was abusive and beat him and his siblings. His father disappeared, and social services came and took all the children. His brother went into the service, his sister went to live with a friend of his mothers and he ended up back in a gang. One night another gang came into their neighborhood and they started a turf war. One of the other gang members made some remark about Elisha's mother, and he went berserk. He started beating this kid with all the anger he had built up over his life. He would have killed that kid if some others hadn't pulled him off the guy. You see Joshua; your life could just as easily have been this guy's life but God found it in His grace to place you in a better place. This man's name was Elisha and it means 'God is Savior'. Joshua your name means 'Jehovah is salvation', so I think there is a purpose for you also." With that said Thomas Johnson decided he had given this young man something to think about and would leave the rest to God. Maybe he would have another opportunity to speak with him in the future.

"I want to thank you for your time Mr. Johnson but I think I have to be going. I have your e mail and your number. If I need to talk again, I will call you." With that Joshua got up and put some money on the table and exited the restaurant feeling he had made a trip to the city for nothing, Mr. Johnson was a nice man but that wasn't what he was expecting when he came. He hadn't expected to hear about some kind of savior that would save his soul. He had to remember to find a drug store and buy the items he wanted in his pocket for the dance, just in case he got lucky.

"Call me anytime son; I'll be here if you need someone to talk to," he hollered after Joshua as he was leaving.

On the perimeter Rafael was disappointed that his charge had not made the right decision this day, but he knew there would be another day. He stood down from his station and un-furrowed his wings and with lightning speed headed for home-base.

Chapter 11

Sixteen years is a long time to be away from family. Jeremiah had enlisted in the Marines a young, angry man. He was tall, physically fit, weighing a hundred and eighty five pounds; he was muscular from years of Marine discipline. He was lighter skinned than most African Americans. He wore his hair short by Maine standard and he had a smile that could disarm a recruit before giving him a harsh reprimand. He was handsome by every accounting. He did his basic training at Quantico, Virginia and struggled at first with authority. His father had always been abusive when he was at home, and he tended to stay as far from him as he could, knowing in a few days he would be gone again. The anger he harbored seemed to drive him to be a good Marine, and after basic, he was shipped off to Germany, then on to Iraq. His career took him from Sergeant to Lieutenant where he led a troop of Marines into battle. There had been a road side bombing that had taken the lives of three of his men. The shock had taken him back to a time when he wanted God to intervene and help his mother, and that always brought him back to being angry and depressed. Years couldn't wipe out the hurt he had harbored from his past, and any incident could bring it to the surface. He drank when not on duty and fought whenever anyone pushed him but he was a good Marine and a good leader.

While on a patrol in Bagdad, following a road side bombing a sniper had taken down one of Jeremiah's men. Tommy was only eighteen and too young to die, Jeremiah thought. Trying to carry him to safety he found himself praying, not from selfish needs or in a drunken stupor. He prayed with earnest for another human being just because he cared and knew he couldn't do anything else. Maybe this time God would listen. "God please save this young man, he has never done anything but try to be a good soldier and a good son." Jeremiah was not aware that this prayer went to the throne-room of God and that the watchers were on standby to come at a moment's notice. Two angels were dispatched to earth and helped Jeremiah carry Tommy to a safe location. Jeremiah didn't know they were angels. They were men dressed like locals; with turbans on their heads, long robes and sandals. These men came from who knew where. They took Tommy into their arms and helped Jeremiah reach the safety of a bunker that had been set up fifty yards away. When they had reached safety, Jeremiah had turned to thank the two men, but to his surprise, they were nowhere to be found.

"That's funny; I swore they came in here with me. Hey Joe did you see two locals come in here?" Jeremiah asked.

"Yes, we saw them, but when we turned around they disappeared. They sure are quick these locals. They blend in with the countryside right before your eyes. That's why it's so darn hard to fight this friggen war. You never know who is who or where they are," one of the medics replied.

"This guy gonna be okay?" said Jeremiah to the medics who were working on Tommy.

"Yeah, you got him here in the nick of time. If you hadn't arrived when you did, and if we didn't get the blood stopped, he would have bled to death. We'll have him patched up in no time, maybe he'll even get sent home," the medic said.

The medics had arrived at the same time Jeremiah and the two locals helping with Tommy had. It made Jeremiah feel something miraculous had happened and maybe God was watching.

"Well one for God, finally. Thanks Lord for the help in this one," Jeremiah said under his breath.

Over the years he had thought of his family, wondering what had ever happened to them. He heard that Elisha had gone to prison; Trinity had gone to college. He never knew what had become of the youngest brother. He vowed one day when he got through with this war and if he survived it, he would go home and try to find his family.

Chapter 12

Elisha was in a Correctional Institution in Florida where he was finishing the last of his ten year sentence for beating up a gang member whom had almost died. The beating had made the young boy lose mobility in one of his legs and he was confined to a wheel chair, totally dependent on his family for his needs. He had gone to the parole board a couple of times but the young boy he had beaten always showed up and the board denied his release. In juvenile detention, Elisha had only become more violent and more aggressive, but going to prison taught him that he wasn't as tough, wasn't as smart, and wasn't as important as he had come to believe himself to be. Elisha was well built, weighed a hundred and fifty pounds and stood five foot nine. He had large biceps from hours of lifting weights and exercise. He had mocha colored skin and strong facial features. He let his hair grow and wore it in dreads locks, always pulled back with a string. He had become a handsome man. In juvenile detention he formed a gang and became the leader. He had ruled with intimidation and threats but when he moved to prison, there were others who were more powerful than he was. Elisha found that without his little group of thugs, he wasn't as strong or as important. When he entered prison, he was housed with a black man who had been incarcerated for ten years and knew how to survive in the prison system. That man took Elisha under his wing and began to teach him the ropes of prison life. Thomas Johnson knew a hurting young black man when he saw one and this one was really no different from any others. Elisha had become a model prisoner after he left juvenile detention and becoming roommates with Thomas Johnson. Thomas made a decision to follow God while doing his time. He had been active in the chapel, working directly with the chaplain. He felt he had been saved from all the anger and hate that had been in his life from years on the inside and when he used to be on the streets. He was changed into a God-chaser in prison. God had shown him how to relate to these young black men, and Thomas had made a commitment in his heart to devote the rest of his life helping wherever he could. He knew when he was released he was going to form a ministry that would be devoted to working with young black men, helping them to stay out of places the likes of where he had been.

At first Elisha didn't trust anyone in prison. He had heard a lot of horror stories about becoming someone's bitch, gang beatings and guards abuse, and this was the last thing that he was going to allow happen to him. He had decided that he would find a gang that he could fit into and that would be his protection from the Aryans and the Latinos that tended to run the prisons.

Thomas Johnson had begun to pray for Elisha the first night he was placed in his housing unit. That set into motion work in the heavens as the watchers were put on alert for a young man that had years before given his heart to Jesus in a tent meeting his mother had taken him to. Elisha had long ago put that night in the back of his memories; he had gone in another direction after his mother's death and the beating he had given that young boy who almost died. The night of the beating, Elisha took out all the pent up anger he had been harboring. The anger from his mother dying and leaving him to fend for himself, for his father beating him at the times when he was home, and for lacking the strength to help his family from being torn apart. That young boy he beat had received all his hatred and hurt, and Elisha knew he couldn't take it back. What was done was done.

"Elisha this is a bad place. There is only one place that will protect you, and that is in the Lord. I'm gonna teach you those ways and help you see that God is certainly concerned with you. If you's willing to listen, I's willing to help you while you is in my cell. Whatcha think of that boy?" Thomas Johnson said to Elisha on his first night in C Block cell twenty four.

"Well old man, I don't know if God is interested in anything I have to say or do. I've been a long time away from talken or listening to anything He might have to say. He ain't done nothen for me or mine," said Elisha

"Well boy if you don't get the right protection in here you is going to be in some deep trouble. There is lots of things going on in here. I've been down a long time, but I have found the Lord to be faithful in keepen me safe and I know He can keep you safe too. Believe it or not, I gots lots of respect from the brothers in here, and they know I means business when I talk to God so they just don't mess with me."

"It seems I don't have much choice in the matter since I have a lot of time on my hands and we is bunkies. Go ahead and tell all the stories you wanna. Can't go anywhere so might as well listen," Elisha said and he listened and he learned.

The watchers hadn't forgotten that commitment Elisha had made years ago and they had been on standby to be activated at a moment's notice. That moment came when Mr. Thomas Johnson began to pray for this young man, whom he could see had so many hurts and pains in is life from years of incarceration, and injustice. He knew a young man in need when he saw one and he knew exactly what this young man Elisha needed and thanked God for placing Elisha in his cell.

Mr. Johnson thought to himself, 'I especially like the name Elisha. It means God is savior, and that is what I shall pray for this Elisha, that God will save him.'

Chapter 13

Trinity, at thirty two, was a successful black woman. She carried herself with an air of confidence. She had dark chocolate skin, weighted a hundred and twenty five pounds and was five six. She kept her hair styled medium length and curled. She had attended the University of Florida on a grant and worked hard to maintain a 4.0 average. She received her master's degree in psychology and had decided to become a social worker. Although years earlier she had vowed never to return to the sub's and ghettos of the cities, Trinity saw that doing so would better serve her life than going on to attain wealth and prestige in a life that couldn't benefit humanity. She had chosen however to live in a small community outside of the city and would commute when necessary. Her mother taught her to be a proud black woman that could do anything she put her mind to. She had encouraged her schooling. Trinity actually liked school; it was a place to escape from the hurt and pain of home whenever her father showed up. She remembered hiding under the bed just so her father couldn't find her when he went into his rants and raves. She had vowed in those hidden times never to marry a man that was abusive and never would she allow her children to be subjected to it. Now, at thirty two she still had not married, she just couldn't take the chance. She didn't always trust herself to be objective when it came to men. She dated, but never let a man get too close. She always had a feeling they had an ulterior motive for liking her and would find excuses to break the relationship off. She took a position with the social service office and began taking on multiple case loads. She was good at what she did as she could zero in immediately if there was abuse in a family. She would be the first to yank children from those homes. She found herself looking into the eyes of young black boys who could have been her brother's. Seeing these young lives always made her vow to find out what happened to her family, but with an overload of cases, she never seemed to find the time. She knew Elisha was still in prison and had told herself many times she would go and visit him but never seemed to get up the courage to go. She might see her father in him and that would ruin their relationship. She knew Jeremiah had joined the Marines but had long ago lost any contact with him. Then there was the baby. The baby her mother was going to call Joshua. He had come into the world and changed all of their lives forever. 'I wonder whatever became of my baby brother,' she thought to herself as she approached the house of a client where she heard a baby crying. 'Don't worry baby, I'm here to help and protect you if that's what you need,' she said to herself as she knocked on the door. 'I have become the protector of the innocent,' she thought 'and I'll do my best til the day I die doing it'.

Chapter 14

Joshua had returned home in time to get ready for the last football game of the season. They were playing a rival school and had beaten them by only a few points their last game. Tonight's game was really crucial to how they ended the season. Joshua was the only black player at Somerset, making it an unusual team. His team respected him and treated him like a brother. That had seemed his only normal relationship while in high school, except for his relationship with Patricia Forrester. He liked playing football, his team made him feel accepted for who he was. Tomorrow night would be the dance, the end to the season. If they won their game, everyone would be excited about the dance. Joshua had decided that the dance would be a turning point with his relationship with Patricia and he wanted it to be a special time.

Saturday afternoon Joshua stopped to get the corsage for Patricia and change into his tux. He was running late but would have just enough time to meet Trish at the dance.

As he thought about this night, he couldn't help but wonder if it would turn out the way he had envisioned. He felt in his pocket to make sure the condoms he had purchased earlier in the city were there and fingered them in anticipation. He knew some of the football team members were going to have alcohol and maybe even some other stuff. Since he had never really partied, maybe tonight would be a good night to relax and just go with the flow. He had always been pretty principled in his belief system about doing drugs or even drinking, but tonight was different. It was a time for a young man to make decisions, his decisions for his life. 'Out with the old; on to the new' he thought.

He had the impression Patricia wanted to be closer in their relationship and maybe tonight was the night to go for the gold. He had gotten some advice from a buddy about the condoms. He had said "make sure you use them right but be sure to use them." They were tucked in his pocket and he was ready to meet the challenge of the night. The first challenge would be is parents who would want to take pictures and give him advice and smoother him with compliments about how great he was and how handsome he looked in his tux. He had only wished he felt that way. He felt a little guilty deceiving them about going to see Mr. Johnson and trying to find out more about his family. They had been keeping him in the dark about it and did not want to discuss it.

"Well handsome, let's get this show on the road," he said to himself in the mirror.

As he came into the living room, his mother began the rhetoric with 'you look so handsome, all the girls will be chasing you, be careful and don't do anything you will regret and don't forget to come home on time.' 'Yea, yea,' Joshua thought. 'I've gotta get out of here.'

"No mom, I'll be fine and I will have fun. Don't worry about me. Patty is going to meet me at the dance, and I will get home on time". With that said he made a quick almost run for the door to escape. He had other plans for tonight, and he certainly wasn't going to discuss those plans with his parents.

"Bye, see you tomorrow. Please don't wait up for me okay? I'll fill you in on all the details tomorrow," he said. With that, he almost ran out the door, got into the car, and sped off toward the school.

In the heavenly realm, the fallen watchers were preparing for a night of mayhem and destruction. "If this kid does what he is planning on doing, we will be able to have a heyday with him. This could be the beginning of the end for this one," one of the fallen said, with a snarl in his voice and hatred dripping from his lips.

The righteous watchers were also waiting to see what decisions tonight would bring to their charge. This young man had been marked for greatness by the Lord himself. By his mere being alive, his gifts would change the lives of many.

    The angels watched and waited as the evening began to unfold. This could be a night of passage they all thought.

Chapter 15

Patricia was waiting in the lobby with some of her friends and some girls who had come to the dance alone. They all had planned on hooking up during the evening even though they had come alone. They didn't plan on leaving alone. When Patricia saw Joshua, she rushed to meet him and practically threw herself into his arms.

He had spotted her immediately among the girls. She stood out from the other girls by her beauty. Her three inch heels made her legs look long and sleek. Her blonde hair, which she usually wore in a ponytail, was cascading down her shoulders in soft waves. She wore a blue dress that accentuated her figure. She was petite with a nice figure. Her dress was fitted through the waist with a slight flare at her hips, and the strapless top accentuated her full breasts. She wore makeup that made her face come alive. As he approached, her he took in the beauty before him. As he got closer, he felt a stirring in his loins. He had been fantasying about this night for weeks.

"I was beginning to think that you were going to stand me up and leave me to fend for myself tonight. Where have you been?" she asked.

"I was just running a little late and making our plans for tonight. It took a little longer than I thought to get away from my parents, and I had to get your corsage," to which he handed it to her with a smile that said "did I do it right?"

"You didn't have to do this but they are beautiful and I will wear them proudly tonight," she said smiling back.

"Let's get this night rolling. Could be a lot of fun or could be the challenge of our year," he said taking her arm and putting it through his.

They presented their tickets at the table to the chaperones before going into the gymnasium where the dance was set up. Some of the chaperons were eyeing them to make sure they didn't do anything that was going to cause a disturbance tonight. Mixed race dating was frowned on and they knew it could be a problem with some of the parents or some of those who were attending the dance tonight. There had been some complaints over the years from parents expressing concern about Joshua Hardgrave attending their school. The administration had always been able to quell all the talk mostly because Mr. Hardgrave was an attorney with a good legal practice in the community.

The room had been decorated by the junior class. They had streamers hung from the ceiling and the lights were low. There were tables with refreshments, and the music was blaring from the speakers. The committee had arranged for music from a group of former students that had formed a band during their senior year and had continued on after. They played at local clubs and functions around the area and vowed to return for the home-coming dance.

"They are actually pretty good, don't you think?" Patricia said, after entering the room.

"Not bad. You wanna dance or just hang out?" he asked.

"Let's dance and see how the evening plays out." She took his hand and led him to the dance floor.

The music had changed to a slow song. Joshua reached for her hand, and at that moment, they got an electrical shock. It seemed funny, and they both laughed but to Patricia it was what was happening to her on the inside. As he drew her in close, she rested her head on his shoulder. He had a rugged physique, and with her three inch heels, her head fit nicely on his shoulder. His arms encircled her and made her feel very safe. She snuggled close to him as the music played. Their fingers entwined, and they moved as one on the floor.

"Your perfume is intoxicating," Joshua said. "You look beautiful; this is a whole other side of you I've never seen before." He gave her that mischievous look with that smile that melted her heart.

She smiled up at him, "Well thank you Mr. Hardgrave. You look pretty dashing yourself. I've been saving this side of me for this special night." Then she snuggled in closer to his body. This was sending an uncontrollable surge in his loins and made him a little self-conscious. She might notice his body's physical, involuntary movements. He decided against worrying about it as she seemed to be enjoying their closeness.

The school had become more liberal over the years; however there were always some students whose families were from the old school and had been raised on prejudice and hatred. They hated to see the races mix, and they always seemed to be at any function that would draw a crowd. As soon as Patricia and Joshua entered the dance floor they felt the stares of a group of students who were hanging out in the corner of the room.

Some of those in the group didn't attend Somerset but they always seemed to get invited to events likes these. There was a select group at Somerset whose families had been raised in the area for many years. These white families, and their generations past, had grown up with the prejudice toward any race accept their own. Some had even owned slaves back in the day and some families where known members of The KKK. The Klan hadn't been active and hadn't caused any significant commotion in several years. Everyone knew they were there, and everyone tolerated the fact they were in the area. As long as they didn't rise up and try to cause any damage, everyone would rather just ignore them than confront them. Tonight however might change the course of the school, the county, the state and especially the future of one young black man who was dancing with a white girl in Klan territory.

Chapter 16

"Let's see if we can get them to come to the party we have set up at the Drinker House," Roy, one of the boys hanging out in the corner said.

"We'll have some drinks with our special recipe. Then maybe we can get them away from here and give them a special talken to," said Ken Johnston. Ken was a senior, who had gotten into Somerset because his grandfather had been a member of the local Order of the Knights, a group that had formed in the 1940's and had a long standing in the community. The group did a lot of social events and kept the community enriched with historic events. Ken always seemed to be in trouble. He had a feeling of entitlement and liked to push his weight around. Ken had joined an underground group with some local skinheads. The school was not aware of his extracurricular activities or the things he had been engaged in for the last few years. The boys that were not from Somerset had been invited by Ken Johnston as some of his friends. Ken was a very persuasive student with a charming way about him when need be. The boys he had invited liked to call themselves Skinheads of the Underworld. They had tattoos mixed with skulls and crossbones and some even had swastikas. They weren't like the KKK of old; these were the new generation of prejudices but with the same agenda of hate. While attending dances or other events, they would have their tattoos and markings covered so they could gain entrance. Some of the more rebellious girls at the school liked having them there to flirt with. This was their way of showing others they could do what they wanted to.

Some had families that were more inclined to the separatist thinking and seemed to enjoy the danger of their company.

"We need to wait awhile. They just arrived. It will seem suspicious if we all leave after just getting here, and we can wait. We have the whole evening. Let's just have some fun while we're here," Ken said.

The evening was progressing. Everyone seemed to be having a good time. Some of Joshua's football buddies were whooping it up with their dates. Winning their last game had put them in a party mood. The chaperones had to ask them to quiet down which only made them more obnoxious. The chaperones finally decided to leave them alone as long as no one was getting hurt, even though some of their dancing and antics seemed a little raunchy for a high school dance. They were only there to make sure no one got hurt and there wasn't any alcohol or drugs at the dance, or so they thought. To the best of their knowledge they hadn't seen anyone come in with any illegal substances, and they assumed they were doing a good job of chaperoning.

It was almost ten p.m. and it seemed some of the participants were getting a little rowdy. The chaperones kept checking the punch to make sure no alcohol had been added so they knew that couldn't be the problem. Some of those in attendance had gone to use the rest rooms but that too was normal with drinks and food. The chaperones were unaware that earlier in the day some of the team had stashed some alcohol in the restrooms. Even some of the girl's had gotten involved in the bathroom stash and supplied the girl's room with drinks. Patricia had entered the restroom a couple times and had decided to try some of the special punch. Joshua had also gone to the restroom and found some of his football buddies encouraging him to try the brew they had brought. Tonight he was going to go against all of his convictions and try to let out the person that he thought was hiding somewhere within him.

Joshua and Patricia were chatting in the corner when Ken Johnston approached and asked if they wanted to go to a party after the dance. Everyone was invited and they would have some good stuff there and lots of fun. Ken knew how to convince people to do things they ordinarily wouldn't consider. He had a large following both Josh and Patricia knew, and although they never really associated with him and his group of friends, they never found them to be too offensive. They told him they would try to make it.

"I don't know Josh. We don't hang out with those guys, and they seem a little too creepy at times. Maybe we should just go find a place to be alone." Patricia didn't have a good feeling about these guys, and she had heard stories about some of them and their families.

"Why not, they can't be that bad. Everyone was invited. We can go check it out and if we don't like it, we can head out," Joshua said. "Come on, the party is just beginning. Let's go have some fun." Joshua was feeling the effects of the drinks. He had given his will over to have a good time without worrying about the consequences, and he just wasn't able to think that far ahead. He thought, what could happen? He had his football buddies and Patricia who liked him, his parents who trusted him and Thomas Johnson said he had a privileged life so why not have a little fun taking this journey, the journey he had vowed to begin tonight.

"Okay but if I feel uncomfortable you have to promise to take me home," she said rather reluctant to go.

"It's a promise!" Joshua said, giving her that mischievous smile.

Before leaving he got together with Joe, his football buddy. He wanted to know if the guys from the team were going to the Drinker House.

"I'll find out from the other guys, and we should meet you out there in a half hour," Joe said. Joe wasn't aware that Ken Johnston was the one behind who had invited Joshua, or he would have told him not to go. He didn't trust Ken or any of the guys he hung with. He had a run in with Ken Johnston in his sophomore year. Ken had invited him to a party and when he got there found it to be a meeting about racism and separatism. Some of the guys that were there had tattoos and shaved heads, and the whole thing made him sick. He vowed never to have anything to do with Ken Johnston again. The football team was a pretty close knit group. They won most of their games over the seasons they had been together, and they were a group who backed one another up. Color had never been an issue with any of them. They were a team, and a team stuck together to be winners.

In the dark recesses, the fallen were howling, ranting and raving. They were arguing with one another as to who would be the one to inflict the first blow. They were bragging about who was the greatest, who had done the worst deeds, and who was going to be the one whose temptations tonight would win a battle.

The righteous watchers were also observing; they however were calling the troops to attention. They would indeed be busy tonight, as soon as someone began to pray to put them into action. They could move at a moment's notice to rescue and protect their charges. They watched and waited, sometimes with dismay at the decisions their charges were making, watching the direction their decisions were taking them, going in the opposite direction for their destiny was always a concern. This would be a night to be on guard. They knew the fallen ones were roaming the area looking to find someone to use and destroy.

Chapter 17

In a small church on the outskirts of town was a group of ministers and prayer warriors that had been called to action by the local chaplain of the jail. They had been meeting together like this for seven years praying for their county and their township. The chaplain had gotten word from an inmate that had recently been incarcerated that, there was going to be some unusual activity during the school dance. Being concerned the chaplain had called a special meeting to pray and intercede for those who would be attending the school dance. They weren't aware of the magnitude of this night but they knew prayer would be of benefit.

"I want to thank you for all coming here tonight," the chaplain opened the meeting. "I believe we have to do some prayer warfare for our young people. I heard that there might be some racial activity happening at the school of Somerset tonight and that someone might get hurt. Now we haven't had anything like this in many years. It doesn't mean that it couldn't happen. We all know that there are those in our county that have prejudice and hatred in them and would like to spew their venom onto our area. Tonight we need to intercede like never before. We do not want any of our children caught in some kind of hate war and we do not want anyone to get hurt, or worse yet hung. I want us to be fervent in our prayers and ask God to protect all those who go out tonight." The chaplain didn't relish using the word hung: It stuck in his throat, and he had to cough to get it out. He hoped no one asked more. He could hardly believe it himself when he had heard it, so repeating it made him uncomfortable. However this night he wanted them to pray with purpose and conviction. They all began to pray at once, offering up prayers for the students that would be out tonight at the dance and anyone who would be out in their county. They prayed fervently and with such determination they could have been heard for miles.

This sent shock waves into the fallen territory. They began to scream and spew venomous words. "How dare they do that? This is our night!" they shouted. These prayers bombarding the heavens sent the fallen angels into confusion and scattered their ranks; leaving many unprotected and defenseless, looking like a cowardly lot.

The righteous came into formation, calling in the rank and file to form a barrier around the county, around the school and around Joshua and his friends. The righteous knew that this was the night that Joshua Lance Hardgrave had been marked for destruction. With the fervent prayer warriors meeting in that little church, the righteous warriors had been activated to go and do warfare in the heavens. To fight the evil schemes of the fallen and to send the cowards back into their haunting ground and to spare this young man and possibly many others. The war was on and the righteous were planning for victory. This little group of prayer warriors knew two things for sure, that God answers prayer and prayer changes things. So the group prayed.

Chapter 18

Joshua and Patricia started towards the Drinker House. The Drinker House had been a home to the Drinker family in the nineteen hundreds. When the Drinkers passed away, the house was eventually converted into a restaurant and party house. It was out in the country on a lonely road lined with old oak trees covered in Spanish moss that gave the whole area an eerie feeling. The food had been good and the setting seemed romantic to some so they turned it into a party house. Many meetings and parties had been held at the house over the years, but as of late it had fallen on hard times and had become a little run down. Some savory groups had been meeting there and the owners had allowed it to keep the establishment running.

"I'm really not comfortable about this, you know that right?" Patricia was getting more and more uncomfortable. She kept looking out the window, staring into the woods and imagining she was going to see something terrible coming out of the trees. All of a sudden a flash of light from the sky exploded on the woods and there hanging from a tree was a noose. She screamed.

"Josh we have to turn around immediately and go," she said almost hysterical.

"What on earth is the matter with you, it is only lightning."

"No Josh I saw something hanging from a tree in the woods. It's a sign, and we need to get out of here, right now." She had sat straight up in the seat and was emphatic that they turn around now.

"Just what did you see in the woods?" He couldn't believe how upset she had gotten just from a flash of lightening.

"I saw a noose hanging from a tree, and that is not a good sign for us to be out here in the middle of the night. You are aware of what something like that means don't you?" She didn't want to bring it up but the facts were there. They were in the neighborhood, it was black and white, they were black and white and they had been personally invited by some very unconventional people. She knew they needed to leave.

"I wanna see that. Where exactly did you see it?" he said as he slowed down and began to back up.

"I don't want to see it again. I want you to turn this car around and get us out of here immediately, please Josh." She was almost crying.

"Okay, okay, I'll turn around but show me where you saw it I wanna see it myself." He had read a lot about such things. He had done a lot of study lately looking up his heritage. He had read about Birmingham, Alabama and Dr. Martin Luther King and some about the KKK, but it had never touched his life because of living with the Hardgrave's and going to Somerset. He knew it was true. How could he have lived so close to things like this and had it miss his life. Was he really protected and blessed like Thomas Johnson had told him he was?

"It was right about here, over there in the woods, turn the car a little that way, and I think you will be able to see it with the headlights." She could feel her heart racing, she knew this to be dangerous and if her parents knew she were here she would be grounded for the rest of her life.

"There, I see it." At once Josh felt a knot in the pit of his stomach. He realized at once that noose was meant for him this night, if not to actually hang him on it, was to scare him enough to get out of Dodge. He knew from instinct that Patricia was right; they needed to vacate this area immediately. Just then they saw headlights coming towards them from the Drinker House direction. He turned the car onto the road and gunned the engine.

"Hang on Patricia, we are out of here." The odometer was hitting 50 in seconds as the car swerved and kicked up dirt. In the distance the other vehicle was coming fast. At the same time headlights were coming at them.

"This doesn't look good, hang on we might have to do some fancy driving to get out of here." He didn't know what was going to happen but he sure wasn't going to get caught and he sure wasn't going to let anyone put a noose around his neck.

He suddenly realized that the vehicle coming towards them was his friend Joe driving his father's SUV with his football buddies coming to see what was happening at the Drinker House. He slowed to a stop and opened his window.

"Hey man, where you going? Thought you were going to a party at the Drinkers, whatsup?" They had already been partying earlier so their mood was already on high.

"I don't think this is where we want to be guys, we are heading home." Josh said a little anxious to leave.

"Hey man this was your idea, what's really going on?"

Patricia blurted out that she had seen a noose hanging from a tree and these guys were known for being in some type of racist gang and they needed to go. There was a vehicle coming down the road fast and it might be them.

"Woe girlfriend, are you serious, a noose?" The guys became serious instantly and noticed the vehicle approaching fast. The pickup truck stopped just behind Josh's car and two very unsavory types exited the truck, they had on leather jackets, tattoos on their heads and necks and one carried a chain in his hand.

"You boys are a long way from home aren't ya?" The largest of the three said.

No one said anything at first; they just stared, the headlights made an eerie sight on this lonely road in the middle of what seemed like nowhere.

"Hey I'm talking to you boy." The large one said to Joshua, nostrils flaring.

"Well we were just leaving bro." Josh said with a little attitude in his voice. He was aware he was scared but he knew he had to show he wasn't.

The three took a step towards the car and by instinct all of those from the football team who were in the SUV emerged at once to form a formation around Josh's vehicle. The movement startled the three and they took a step backwards, almost falling over one another. They regained their composure and assessed the situation. They realized they were outnumbered and that these guys were in good shape, and some were rather large for their age. They had only been sent out as a watch to see if anyone was coming to the Drinkers, and deducing the odds against them winning this battle as slim, they decided to back down and get back in their truck and turn around.

"Wow did you see the likes of those guys, tattoos, leather, and chain's? We coulda whipped their butts," said Harry the linebacker from the team.

"Well I don't wanna know and I don't wanna have to do this again. Let's get out of here before they go and get recruits," Josh said. "Patty and I are going to stop and get something to eat but let's get as far away from here as possible, maybe the next town, closer to home." Josh was physically shaken by the whole ordeal. He knew he was the center of why they were all here getting confronted, and it was all about the color of his skin and being with a white girl. He also knew this situation put Patricia in harm's way, and he didn't want that to ever be the issue. If he thought her parents were upset with her going to the dance with him, they would really be upset that she was put into a situation like the one they just encountered.

"We'll turn around and follow you, let's get out of here." Joe said.

Just at that moment the skies opened up, and it began a torrential down pour. Lightning flashed across the sky and thunder roared. The night had become alive with activity.

In the little church on the outskirts of town the small group of prayer warriors was pounding heaven with their prayers. The righteous were fighting the evil forces of the night. There was a battle going on and angels with swords were flaring them at one another, sending lightning through the sky and thunderous peels. The righteous were prevailing and the fallen were losing ground. Wailing and weeping and gnashing of teeth, the fallen were cursing the righteous and the humans for making them lose the battle of the night.

Chapter 19

The Drinker House had been closed for the season. When the group of young men came saying they wanted to hold a party on prom night to keep kids from drinking and give kids a nice place to hang out, the owners relented, not knowing the men had ulterior motives for this party. The main guests were going to be a couple who shouldn't be seeing one another; any self-respecting person knows whites and blacks shouldn't mix. Their parents had been teaching this to them for years. It had passed down through generations. Some of their great grandfathers had been Exalted Wizards in the Klu Klux Klan. Today the younger generation had their-own form of Klan ideas. They leaned towards the Nazi theory of white supremacy. This thinking was ingrained from years of bigotry. For any to think different, would cause them to be ostracized by their families. Some members had shaved heads or close cropped hair, and body piercings. They wore leather and chains and drove pickup trucks flying the rebel flag. They hung together at a property in the outskirts of town. The property had barbed-wire fencing surrounding the compound and guards stationed at the entrance. No one was allowed they didn't recognize. While others who belong to the group were like Ken Johnston, clean cut, respectable by all outward appearance, conforming to Somerset Academy standards. They wore black shirts and pants with patches and symbols of the broken cross and black boots. This form of dress made them look like an organization that meant business. Under their shirts, they carried the markings of their beliefs and ideologies. They all would come together at secret meetings at the compound.

The look-outs returned to give the news about the car full of big guys who outnumbered them and that the principles got away. They would have to make plans for another day to take care of this business. This angered the leader and he swore and ranted and cursed until they were all in frenzy.

The rain was coming down in torrents and they could hardly see across the yard. Thunder and lightning flashed and boomed all around the house, and they decided there wasn't much they could do so they chose to hang out and just party and tell war stories from the past and try to decide what to do in the future.

Chapter 20

Joshua and Patty arrived a few minutes later than his football buddies. They had found an all-night restaurant open in the next town, and they all filed in joking and patting one another on the back telling how they had run off a bunch of nut jobs.

"No hair, no brains, nothing to hold their brains in place," one of the guys said patting Joe on the back. "You were brave there bro, better watch out, the wrestling team will want you," and they all laughed.

Patricia was the only girl as the guys had abandoned dates in hopes of picking some more seasoned girls at the Drinker House. The kind of girls that they wouldn't take home to mamma but the kind they would party with. Since they never made it to the Drinker House, they were just the guys and Patricia. She was feeling a lot more relaxed with all these hunky guys to protect them.

"I don't think we should brag too much about this," Joshua said. "It seems these guys know their way around, and remember they were at the dance. They somehow have access to our school and where we hang out. Maybe we should try and forget this night." Joshua knew this night was really about him and Patricia being together and he didn't want any of his friends getting caught up into something that seemed dangerous and unexplainable to him at the moment.

"Come on Joshua, we could of beaten their butts man. Maybe we should of, then they wouldn't dare come around anymore." Joe was fiercely loyal and totally aware of what this night was about. He had heard talk before but never broached the subject with Joshua. He would just turn away and not enter into any of the conversations.

"No Joe, I don't want anyone getting into any kind of confrontations because of me. I can take care of myself. I don't' want anybody fighting my battles." This sounded rather heroic and brave, and he knew if they hadn't been there tonight it could have turned out really bad for him and Patricia. "I do want to thank you guys for being there tonight though, it could have turned really nasty and Patricia might have gotten hurt."

"Hey, I'm right here. Remember? We could all have been in trouble if I hadn't seen that noose hanging in the tree. If we had gotten to the Drinker House, who knows what would have been awaiting us. I think someone was watching out for us tonight, and as far as I'm concerned, I'm thankful they were."

After eating and talking about the events of the night, they decided it was time to get home. Joshua had said he would be home at midnight and it was two a.m. already. Patricia hadn't said what time she was supposed to be home and he wondered how he was going to get her home without her parents knowing they had been together the whole evening. They left the restaurant and sat in the car for a short time. Joshua wasn't sure what he was going to do about getting Patricia home yet but he had to come up with a plan before arriving at her door.

"Patricia, I know your parents didn't want you to go with me tonight, and it's too bad you didn't trust me enough to tell me." After the events of this evening, he decided they needed to be completely honest with one another. This could get back to their parents and they needed to know where they stood on the issue.

"I didn't know if you would still have taken me if you knew they didn't want us to be together on a date," she said.

"Well you are probably right, I wouldn't have taken you. That didn't mean I wouldn't have hooked up with you at the dance," he said with a grin.

"I thought you might have asked someone else, and I was afraid of that. I have been waiting for this night all year, and I wasn't going to let anyone spoil it, even if some unplanned events did," she pouted.

"Do you think your parents will be waiting up for you when I take you home?"

"I don't know, sometimes they are awake when I come in but not physically waiting by the door. Tonight I am kinda late, so who knows?"

"This could be rather sticky don't you think? Got any suggestions to keep you from getting in trouble?" He was smiling at her but he also was concerned this could turn out badly. He was more afraid of this next challenge than of the one faced on the road with the thugs.

"There is something else I was waiting for tonight that we never got around to," she said sheepishly. "I was kinda hoping we would take our relationship to another level, starting with a kiss." She couldn't believe she had come out and said it, but she had been waiting so long for this moment that she was going to do whatever it took to make it happen.

Joshua started laughing. "You don't beat around the bush do you? I had planned on taking that step tonight also but things got a little confusing, and heck girl, I haven't even taken you home yet. Can't you wait til the time is right?" He had a full smile now that made him totally irresistible.

Patricia started to blush and he reached over and drew her close to him and kissed her softly on the lips. She couldn't help but respond. She had waited so long and the emotions of the night came flooding through with passion. She wrapped her arms around his neck and kissed him back. The passion went directly to Joshua's loins and he had a hard time holding back all the desires and longings he had been dreaming of for months. Patricia met his passion with her own desires and if it hadn't been for them sitting in the parking lot he would have taken her right there. When they realized where they were and that the lights of the restaurant and other patrons were around, he said they needed to go somewhere more private.

As they drove toward Patricia's home, she snuggled close to him and every part of her wanted to become one with him. She didn't know how or when but she was going to give herself to him, and they would become one, the couple that other's didn't want them to be.

"I think tonight I should just take you home. We can consummate these feelings at another time. It's kind of late, and we're already in trouble." He knew he wanted more but he wasn't sure he could handle all that would come with taking their relationship to the next level. "I'll drive you home, let you out and wait for you to enter the house before I leave and pray that you don't get into trouble." He had made his decision and that was that.

"Okay if you promise to call me tomorrow, but not too early I think I am going to sleep in." She didn't like his decision, but she understood it. The kiss would hold her over until they were together again.

"It's a deal," he said as he rounded the corner to her house. There was a light on the porch beckoning her arrival.

"I'll wait right here, hurry in okay?"

She reached over and took his face and kissed him on the lips then raced from the car to the house. She opened the door and went inside, there didn't seem to be anybody waiting for her.

Joshua reached in his pocket, fingered the package with the condom. 'Guess I'll save this for another day.' He got out his wallet, placed the condom in it and drove away.

Chapter 21

Trinity had an abuse case that took her into the side of town that she wasn't familiar with and didn't like. The mother in her case, Kasandra Jones, had taken a job at a restaurant in a not-so-good neighborhood. Part of her assignment was to see if Kasandra had gotten a job and found an apartment, in hopes of getting her children back. As Trinity approached the restaurant, she noticed it was full.

'Lunch time, I should have come at off-time. I probably won't be able to talk with her,' she said to herself. 'At least I'll see if she is here and working.' She parked her car, locked the doors and entered the packed little restaurant. The sign said they specialized in ribs and pork rinds. 'Haven't had those in a long time,' she thought.

She found a booth towards the back and settled in. From this vantage point she could view the front door and the door to the kitchen; if she is here she should be able to see her. It was noisy with everyone talking and laughing. The restaurant was run down and at the same time had a warm neighborhood feeling. Most of the clientele were middle-aged to seniors, laughing and joking. The front door opened and the little bell rang announcing another patron. Every seat was filled, and a man came walking towards the kitchen door.

"Hi Pops," one of the pretty young waitresses said. "There should be a seat in no time. Just hang out. Something will open up soon." She was pleasant, and this man seemed to be a regular of this little establishment. Trinity thought he looked like a friendly old man and decided to ask him to join her, after all what harm could come from it. This place was packed with people.

"Excuse me Mr. Pops," she said "you can join me if you don't mind. I'll only be here a short time and there doesn't seem to be any seats available," she said trying to look friendly.

"Well don't mind if I do young lady," he said with a shine from his gold teeth that made his face light up when he smiled. He had never seen her here before. She was in her thirties, close cropped hair, very pretty, well dressed like a lawyer, banker or maybe some profession from up-town he assumed. She had a familiarity about here, a look he couldn't put a finger on.

"What's a pretty young thing like you doing in the likes of a place like this? I never seen you in here before," he said.

"Just here on some business," she said.

"Well it is my lucky day then," he said sliding into the booth opposite her. "My name's Thomas Johnson and I'm pleased to meet you missy."

"It is my pleasure, Mr. Johnson. I'm Trinity Lance and I was wondering what's good on the menu?" She was more relaxed and actually glad he had sat down with her. She didn't seem so alone in these unfamiliar surroundings.

"Lance, that's an unusual name in these parts. Once knew a young man with the last name Lance. I met him years ago in another time and place. You don't have any brothers do ya?" he asked, thinking she looked like his young Bunkie back at the prison. "By the way, call me Pops. Everyone around here does."

"Yes I do Mr. Johnson, or Pops. We got separated years ago, and I haven't heard a word about them. I'm sorry to say one got in a bit of trouble and ended up in a juvenile detention center." It was funny how easy it was to talk with this man, he didn't seem judgmental or condemning and since she didn't know him, what difference would it make to share her story. Most of her life, she had been pretty careful to keep that part of her life private.

"Well, this young man's name was Elisha and I met him in prison. He was an angry young man when he came to me, but over time he got himself straightened around." Pops was watching Trinity closely as she seemed to be turning pale and got really quiet.

"Pops that's my brother's name, and he went to prison for a long time for being involved in a gang and almost killing a boy. I can't believe I am sitting here talking to someone who knows him." The air drained from her chest as she sat back in her seat and contemplated the situation before her. She had prayed before entering this neighborhood. She was out of her element and wanted to be strong and do her job with an air of confidence. All of that strength and confidence evaporated sitting before this man called Pops.

The watchers were stationed at the four corners of the restaurant; they had been dispatched by Trinity as well as Thomas Johnson's prayers. Trinity had asked for guidance and protection in this neighborhood, and Mr. Johnson had asked for someone to share his experiences with in order to help them along their walk in life.

"We shall remain here to protect," Ahlai, the leading angel in charge said. He was tall, slim, imposing with light color hair and green eyes. He had a wing span of six feet across on each side and could form his wings to spin in circles if the situation presented itself. The others fell into place with his command. These watchers were warriors. They carried shields and swords. Their battle wouldn't be with humans but with the evil watchers who hide in the shadows, lurking in the streets, ever seeking someone to destroy with their vile temptations.

The fallen that hung in this neighborhood came with the drug pushers and women who prostituted themselves. They would whisper evil thoughts and evil desires of wanton depravity that made humans think they were lost beyond rescue, with no hope. Their ultimate goal was to see them dead.

As Trinity began to tell the story of the Lance family, Pops listened intently. Some of this story he already knew, but this would come from another perspective, one in which he would use to try to bring healing to these two family members and possibly in a time would be able to reunite them when Elisha exited those prison walls.

At the end of her story, Pops smiled and said, "This is a great day Ms. Trinity, the heavens have heard our prayers, and the good Lord is going to reunite your family. This is just the first step. Elisha is going to need someone when he reenters life on the outside. He has been down for a long time and this old world has changed a lot. Hell they didn't even have twittering and tweeten when I was in prison. Twitter's and tweeters were birds, say nothing of all these new fancy gadgets to keep in touch with one another," he gave a robust laugh that made others in the restaurant turn and notice them. "He'll be needen a place to call home and what better place than with family," he said.

Trinity knew this would be true; after all, she was in the business of seeing people put their lives back together and a stable place to live was always at the top of the list. At the same time, this made her a little, heck no, a lot nervous. This was the brother that always had a temper. He could end up being like her father, and she was sure she didn't want to invite this back into her life. She would have to meet him and talk with him and see for herself if what this kindly old man was telling her was the truth.

She got all the information from Pops on where to go and how to see her brother. She would make arrangements right away to travel to the prison and look her brother in the eye, and hope beyond all hope, that he would be more like their mother than their father.

As they were finishing their lunch of ribs, pork rinds and southern yams, Pops said he wanted to tell her a story.

"A few days ago a young man contacted me through my internet site. This internet business is something I heard about while I was in prison and when I got out went to investigating how to use it. Gotta say it has been a blessing to me today. Anyway, this young man wanted to come down here and meet with me. He was a black boy being raised by some white folks. Can you even imagine anything as dumb as something like that? Those white folk hadn't told him nothen about his history. I could see in his eyes he was feelen lost and looken for something about who he was. Said he had been adopted when he was a baby and these folks had put him in some private white school. Can you get the picture how that black boy was sticken out like a sore thumb in that white school, and down here in the south no less? Well anyway, he was looken for some answers to some hard questions. You know how it is when you're a teenager and all them hormones are a letten lose and you wanna know everything and know nothen?" He had thought this young pretty black woman might be just what Joshua Hardgrave needed, after all she was used to working with the hard issues of life and she would be more a mother figure than this old black man. Guess he could be a good Pops to young black boys, but this boy needed to hear from someone who had some class, who had made something in this world and had the training to know how to talk out some hard issues.

"If I can get this young man to contact me again would you be willing to talk with him, maybe give him a little push in the right direction? Let him know that all his liven with them white folks wasn't all bad. He got's a good education, dresses good, drives a pretty fancy car and can go far in this old world if he uses it to his advantage." He kept thinking just maybe this would be the connection he had been praying for concerning Joshua ever since he met him that day. Funny how they had met right here in this little establishment and now God was seeing fit to answer his prayers sending this lady Trinity Lance his way.

"It would be my honor to help Mr. Johnson, Pops. I've devoted my life to trying to help others and it sounds like you have too. If he contacts you again, give me a call." With that she pulled out one of her business cards and handed it to him. "It has been a full day for me meeting you but I guess I should do what I came here to do. Would you know if a Kashandra works here? She is one of my case files, and I need to know if she has gotten herself a job."

Looking around she couldn't see any waitresses. Lunch time had come and gone and so had most of the patrons. It seemed all the waitresses where in the back taking a break.

Pops called, "Kashy you back there worken today?"

With that, Kashandra Jones emerged from the back. She was small, skinny to the point of bones showing through her tight T-shirt. Her hair was matted from working in a greasy restaurant. By all accounts, she had been attractive when she was a teen but her hard life was showing on her at an early age. She had been scurrying around, working hard during the lunch hour. She hadn't even noticed her case worker. Her tables were on the other side of the restaurant and lunch time was a zoo.

"Yeah Pops, I'm here. What can I do for ya," she replied.

Just as she stepped near the table, she was taken aback by the person sitting with Pops. It was her case worker, Ms. Lance.

"Ms. Lance, I didn't see you come in. How long you been here?" she asked.

"Well Kashandra, I have been here way longer than I planned. I just stopped by to check and see if you were following through with getting a job and I ran into a very nice gentleman who offered to sit with me and keep me company during lunch. I am so glad to see you are here working. I'll note that in my records and the next step will be to see that you have a safe place to live. Then we'll work on getting those children of yours back to a stable environment with their mother who loves them. Are you making your scheduled visits to see them?" She knew she had, but she wanted to see her reactions, after all that gave her more insight into a person than the words they said. Trinity had learned at a young age that some people knew how to lie with such a straight face you couldn't be sure if it were the truth or a flat out lie. Her father had been a good teacher in that avenue.

"Yes Ms. Trinity, I see them twice a week at the foster families home where they are. They seem like nice people, and the kids seem to be doing well. I haven't seen their father in over a month and don't know where he, and I hope he stays gone," she said this with a straight face, but Trinity could see something else. She was pretty sure if this guy showed up; Kashandra would jump right back into bed with him and probably get pregnant and have another mouth to feed. Then he would take off again as soon as some young skirt flitted by or he heard about another great deal that would make him a fortune.

"I hope you mean that Kashandra, he has been nothing but bad news for you, hitting you, leaving you pregnant and now without a place to live or money to feed your children. Subjecting them to that kind of abuse sends the wrong message for your children. They begin to live what they see, and to make unwise choices on their own." She knew she was preaching but some of these young girls needed a good preaching to.

Pops agreed and told her no man should be hitten on a woman and if he comes back and try's anything like that to just call him. He'll take care of him.

With that, Trinity decided it was getting late, much later than she had planned on being in this neighborhood and that she should be on her way. She actually gave Pops a hug and told him to be in touch if that young boy ever called and he needed her help. When she got to the car it was still all in one piece and she gave a little "Thank you God for protecting my car, now if you'll just guide me out of here and back home I'll be much appreciative." With that she started the engine and drove her car into the street to head north.

Two of the watchers stationed on Bears Boulevard over the restaurant came to attention and went off with Trinity as she headed through the streets towards the freeway that would lead her home. The other two stayed with Pops as he bowed his head and gave thanks for a very full day in his life.

"Thank you Lord for Trinity Lance. You work things out for your good and I can see now how my meeting young Elisha is a part of a bigger picture in your plans than I could have ever imagined. I will go home and write Elisha this very day and tell him of all the great things you are doing and for him to keep the faith." 'God has a bigger plan for my life than I ever dreamed;' he thought. 'You are going to use me to reunite a family broken by heartache and pain. Yep, right up my alley God.' And he ended his prayers.

With that the two watchers smiled to one another and returned to the heavens.

Chapter 22

The next day after the dance Joshua was deciding whether to tell his parents about the encounter on the road to the Drinker House. If he told them, he would have to explain why he was going there in the first place. He might lose their trust and at the moment that was the last thing he wanted to do. If Patricia's parents found out they had gone to the dance together, they might call his parents and then he would have to come clean so for the time being he was going to keep this from them. There was, however, someone he thought he could talk to about these events, and it was Mr. Thomas Johnson. He waited until noon and called Mr. Johnson to see if he could meet with him again.

Mr. Johnson had gone to church and came home to do some work around his apartment fixing the bathroom pipes that had been clogged, when Joshua called. He was glad to hear from him and happier yet that he didn't have to work on the clogged sink any longer.

"Son I am so glad to hear from you today. What can this old man do for ya?" he said with a smile on his face knowing that God had answered another prayer about them meeting up again.

"Well sir, I had a very unusual incident happen to me last night and I need someone who might be able to explain some things about it to me." He didn't want to tell the story over the phone as he didn't want anyone hearing him tell it, and he really wanted to talk with Mr. Johnson in person.

"Tell you what son, if you want to meet me around two o'clock at the same restaurant we met at before, I'll buy you a late lunch and we can talk for a couple hours and get you back out a here before evening time. How's that sound to ya?" Pops wanted to see him and sooner would be better than later. He would gladly leave his clogged sink and anything else that might want to take his time. After all, it was the Lord's Day and what better day to do the Lord's work on.

"I think that would work for me, I'll see you around two." Joshua hung up the phone and went to find his father to ask if he could use the car to run a few errands before dinner.

"I wanted to ask how the dance went last night son?" said his father.

"It went fine sir. The football team was there and Patricia Forrester came. Those guys who graduated from Somerset that started a band played, and the place was decorated nice. Everyone seemed to have a good time." He wanted to keep it as generic as possible.

"It was a little late when you got in. I thought your mother said to be in by midnight?"

"Yes, it was, some of the guys wanted to go out and get something to eat so we stopped at the BigN's Restaurant for something to eat. It's an all-night restaurant. Time just got away from us. I'm not in trouble, am I dad?" He needed to get the car to go see Mr. Johnson and he wanted to leave soon.

"Guess I can understand how that happens when you're with a bunch of guys, especially football players. I'll talk to your mother. She'll be okay with it. What did you say you needed the car for?"

"I need to go and pick up a few things before school tomorrow, and I said I would get together with Joe later. I will be back before dinner if that's okay?" Again he hated lying to his father; he had always been on his side and always stuck up for him. He just wasn't ready to tell him about Mr. Johnson, and he really wasn't ready to tell him about the altercation on the back road last night or the noose in the tree.

"Okay, I'll clear it with your mother, but make sure you get back here for dinner. She is going to want to hear all about last night and how everyone looked and if you danced with anyone. You know that women kind of stuff?"

Joshua grabbed his jacket and headed for the car. It would take him a little time to get to the city but traffic on Sunday was slow so he should make it in plenty of time.

Chapter 23

Patricia wasn't going to hear from Joshua the next day and maybe never again. When she got home, her father was waiting to talk with her. He knew she had been at the dance with Joshua and somehow he knew about the incident on the road. She couldn't figure out how he could know that. Joshua wouldn't have told him, and she couldn't believe any of the football players would have given her up. Her father wouldn't tell her how he knew. She was given a harsh talking to and said they would discuss this the next day.

When Patricia lay in bed she kept going over and over in her head how her father could have known about the dance and the encounter. She heard her father in the next room talking with her mother and she heard him say "She is never going to see that nigger again and that is the end of it." She couldn't hear what her mother replied and then the door slammed. Patricia couldn't believe what she had just heard. Almost immediately memories came flooding into her mind. When she was nine she had heard her father come home late one night angry and loud. She had snuck out of bed and lay at the top of the stairs, and she saw her father and another man arguing over something that had happened earlier in the evening. He had used that same word, saying that should teach him a lesson he wouldn't forget. The other man had used the word wizard and then they went into the kitchen and closed the door. Patricia wasn't nine anymore and she knew a lot more about the racial issues in the area than her family would have believed. She was not racist and didn't believe anyone else should be either. The realization that her father was a racist, made a knot form in her stomach. She was becoming physically ill thinking her father could in some way be connected with those people they had met on the road. She lay awake for a long time trying to put the pieces together when she finally fell asleep around four in the morning.

Chapter 24

Rafael was setting up the perimeter around the restaurant with his regiment the same as before when Joshua and Thomas Johnson had first met; only this time with more vigilance for the evils had been angered as of late. 'Perhaps today my young friend, perhaps today' said Rafael. After Thomas Johnson had sent up a prayer for Joshua, Rafael had immediately gone into protect mode and called upon assistance to secure the area from the fallen.

The fallen were caught off-guard. It seemed to always throw them into confusion, when people began to pray at a moment's notice.

"Get to that restaurant and try to cause a diversion," said the lead evil. We cannot let that Johnson guy talk about Jesus." Uttering the name Jesus caused him to choke. As they tried to form rank, they cursed and screamed at one another as to who was going to do what. When they reached the restaurant, they found the righteous were already around the perimeter and the evils were held back by sword and shields. Realizing they were out-ranked, they fell back into the recesses of darkness in the alleys around the neighborhood.

Chapter 25

Joshua made the trip in record time, and found Pops waiting in the same booth they had sat in the last time they met. 'Must be his personal booth,' he thought as he slide in.

"Why you looken so tired today son? What you been up to?" Pop's asked eyeing him.

After ordering something to eat, Joshua began telling Pops about the night before. When he got to the part about the noose in the tree, Pops became intensely interested and leaned in closer to hear. He didn't think sharing this information with the others in the restaurant would be beneficial as it could easily turn into a riotous atmosphere. The men who hung out in this establishment were well aware of racial issues. Some of the older men had lived when they couldn't even enter a restaurant where white folk were. They were well ready to give opinions and get riled up while doing it.

"Son this is extremely dangerous what you are telling me. Do you think that noose was hung there for you?"

"I believe it was, I believe we were setup to go out to that house, and they were waiting for us. If Patricia hadn't seen it before we got there, I don't know what would have happened. What do you think this all means?" Joshua asked.

"You must know that racism is alive and well. Although people want to brush it under the rug in this day and age, it is still very active. You going to a dance with that white girl must have set them off. Even though you have been friends with this gal all these years, you actually dating her and maybe getting intimate with her wasn't acceptable in their eyes. Have you told your parents about this?"

"No sir, I am not sure how they would handle it and then I would have to divulge some other information of why I was going out there anyway." Joshua said a little reluctant.

"Well this is bigger than you being reprimanded for not being where you were supposed to be. This is a life and death thing son. You need to tell them. They might be targeted for their role in raising you and letting you go to that school and getting too friendly with one of their white girls." Pops was dead serious. He had seen things like this happen before. He even knew a man that got beat up so bad you couldn't recognize him, just for going to a white woman's house to help fix a broken furnace. They thought he was there to do her harm and wouldn't even listen to the woman trying to explain. Had hit her a few times too, and told her to shut up.

"What do you mean life and death and how would they target my parents? They weren't doing anything wrong?" Joshua had never thought about his parents being harmed.

"Son, racism isn't rational. The folks that think that way are ignorant and unlearned. Some of them has learned it from their parents and it's passed on down through their generations. Because they don't think right they blame anyone that is associated with one of us. Your parents need to know. They sound like reasonable, caring folks, and they need to have the heads up."

"I guess when I get home, I better tell them, but I know there is going to be hell to pay for my disobeying them last night." He dropped his head. This was going to become a big deal after all he thought.

"If that's all you gets is grounding or taking away the car to save some lives, then it is worth it." Pops was trying to be gentle but firm about what Joshua needed to do. He knew the severity of this kind of situation. He had seen racism to this extent many times in prison and heard talks by his family in the past about hangings of young black men for just being in the wrong place at the wrong time.

"What does it mean, that noose in the tree?" Joshua finally said, lifting his head and looking Pops directly in the eyes.

"It means they were giving you a message to stay in your place. It is a symbol of the hate in their hearts and the hanging of black folk for being who God created us to be. You are learning a lesson about your heritage, and I believe that is why you came to talk to me in the first place. You wanted to learn who you were."

"Well I know about racism. I don't live in a bubble. I have felt it from time to time growing up. When my parents would take me places and people would look at me different from the other kids that were there. I have always known I am different, but I kind of started thinking it made me unique instead of hated. My parents were really good at protecting me like that. I have always wondered, however, if I knew my real family would I feel the same way? Would being around all black people make me feel complete?"

"Well Joshua, being complete isn't about color. It is about who you know and who you choose to serve in your life. Remember when I told you God wanted you to know Him? This is exactly what I was trying to get across to you. He wants to be your Father, your family. He wants you to be His son and there ain't no color in His family. The color He is looking at when He sees us is the color of the blood of Jesus and that is red."

"To tell the truth, I was doing some praying last night, when I saw that car beating down on us and wasn't sure if we were going to get out of there or not. I started asking God to get us out of there." he said sort of sheepishly.

"And He did, didn't He? That is exactly what I am talking about, He wants us to pray and talk to Him, and He wants to help us when we are in need."

The righteous angels were all standing at attention. They knew that what Mr. Johnson was saying was truth, and they always held the truth in highest esteem.

"Hold your ranks steeds. The fallen are lurking around looking for someone to devour, but truth will prevail today," Rafael said with a commanding voice.

"Joshua, your life is not your own. The Lord has given you this life to honor Him. He has given you a chosen destiny, and He will help you to be all He created you to be, but first you have to bow to His will and give your life over to Him," Pops said.

"How do I do that Pops?" Joshua asked a little reluctant.

"Look, years ago someone came to me with that same statement. He said 'Johnson, you been trying to run your own life all these years and look at the mess you got it into. You're not doing such a good job of it are you?' I had to admit I wasn't, and I was at the place where I was questioning a lot of things in my life and the world, sorta like where you are at today. Anyway, he suggested that I give God a chance, ask Him to be real to me and ask Him into my life. Well, that didn't seem like a big deal, so I said why not. What the heck, everything up to this point wasn't that good. So I bowed my head with him and said a short prayer and asked Jesus to be real to me and to come into my life. Joshua, my life has never been the same. I have never had a bad day since. I have had hard days. I have had tough days, but never have I had a day I can't get through. God put a peace inside of me that I can't even begin to explain to you, but it is real and He can do the same thing for you. God can answer all of your questions and lead you to the truth of what you are looking for. You just have to trust Him." With that said Pops stopped to let Joshua process what he had told him.

After a few minutes of thought Joshua said, "Do you think this is what I should do Pops? I sure could use that kind of peace in my life, and I really do want the answers to my questions."

"Yes Joshua that is what God wants you to do, and it would be an honor and privilege to pray with you to know that. All you have to do is believe in your heart and confess with your mouth that Jesus Christ is Lord. Let's pray." With that Thomas Johnson bowed his head and asked Joshua to do the same and they prayed to ask Jesus into their hearts.

On the perimeter there was jubilee. The angels were dancing and singing and praising God. Their charge had accepted the challenge and he had given his life to God. They would now be on alert to help him find his destiny, the destiny God had prepared for him.

"Joshua, I want you to be aware that this doesn't mean that your life is going to be perfect from this day forward. There will still be challenges and trials but it means that God is going to help you work through them.

He is going to always lead you to the truth, and it is the truth that will continually set you free. I believe you are going to find the meaning of the noose, and you are going to know what to do regarding your relationships and your family. I will continue to pray for you that He will lead you on the path to the fulfilling life you have been created for. You must promise me you will tell your parents about the dance, the noose, and that you are looking for answers to your true family identity. Will you do that?"

"Yes I promise I will and will you keep praying for me as I know I am going to be in big trouble?" he said with a grin on his face for the first time since they began talking.

"There is one more thing I would like you to do," he said reaching into his pocket for the card Trinity had given him. "There is a lady I met a while ago who works for social services. She is a black lady, and I think talking to her will give you some balance and maybe help you find the truth. Her name is Trinity Lance, and if you like I will call her and see if the two of you can meet up. I think she lives near you so you can find a place to get together without driving to the city. I'll call her tomorrow and you call me late in the day and I will tell you where to meet." Pops was sure this was the right connection. There was something about her story and Joshua's that seemed to connect. He was sure this was a God appointment. "Here is her card. I have written the number down so you can keep her card, but let me make the connection for you since I have something to tell her anyway." Pops wanted to be kept in the loop on this one; it seemed there was a lot at stake.

"That sounds fine if I am not grounded for life and if I can get away." With that they both laughed, and Joshua said he would call tomorrow later in the day.

The fallen were screeching, shaking with fear. Their leader was going to punish them for failing to fulfill their mission to destroy Joshua Lance Hardgrave. Their leader hated to lose. His mission was to steal as many souls as possible and those working for him knew he was relentless in is mission. They would be tortured and tormented, cast into utter darkness for their failures. They argued amongst themselves, blaming one another and lying to save their sorry beings.

The righteous were leading the way for Joshua to return home. They knew it would be a test for him to share his heart with his parents. They also knew it was way over due, and his parents needed to know what his life was really like being black in a white world.

On the way home, Joshua thought about Patricia. She had been really scared when she saw the noose in the tree and was really afraid when the car with those guys pulled up. If she hadn't been insistent on leaving and getting out of there; if she hadn't seen the noose; he wasn't sure what would have happened to them last night. He would call her when he got home. He needed to know if she was okay.

Chapter 26

Trinity Lance had attended church and was catching up on paperwork when the phone rang. She was surprised to hear Pops on the line. She wasn't sure if she would see him or hear from him again after that day in the restaurant. It had simply been a casual meeting that turned into a big revelation about her brother Elisha. He had also explained about a young black boy named Joshua Hardgrave that had come to see him and Pops had asked her if she could find a time to meet with this young man. He didn't need her social service expertise but did need an ear and a woman of color to speak with. She was intrigued by the fact that he had been raised by a white family and attended a white school. Pops filled her in about the noose in the tree and meeting the men on the back road, she was sure she wanted to speak with him.

"Set it up Pops. I will arrange my schedule to accommodate this young man on Tuesday, and it will be my pleasure. How are you doing, and have you heard from Elisha? I plan on going to see him next week. I'll tell him you said hi." She had put off going to see Elisha but felt this call from Mr. Johnson was the push she needed to go and do what she knew was right.

"I told him I spoke with a young lady the other day by a chance meeting and explained his story but I didn't think it my place to tell him who you were, I thought maybe you would want to do that yourself." Pops had written Elisha right away after meeting Trinity but had decided it was out of his realm of responsibility to say it was his sister. After all, he didn't know if she was going to accept him and didn't want Elisha to lose hope.

"I will let you know how the meeting with this young man goes and if you don't mind, I'll call and tell you what happened after I have seen Elisha. I must tell you I am a little apprehensive. It has been a long time. He was so much like my father, angry all the time, and the gang he hung with was so cruel." She was being honest about her feelings. She had put her family in the back of her mind for so long, concentrating on her own life, but now she was also beginning to feel that she needed that connection of closeness that only family could bring.

"I'll be prayen for you for both meetens, and I know you'll do just fine. You have a good head on your shoulders." He was sure she had what it took to put things together and make things right. "I'll call back tomorrow with the time. Is there any special place you want to meet?"

"How about The Pizza Palace at three o'clock in the village, should be quiet and not many people there at that time so we can talk without interruption. I'll be home all day, but if I am not, leave a message on my machine and I'll get it."

Pops said he would make the arrangements and call her to let her know. With that said and a short prayer to thank God for all He was doing to bring healing to these families, he decided to write Elisha again.

Chapter 27

When Joshua arrived home his parents were out so he decided to call Patricia and see how she was doing after their eventful evening. The phone rang several times before a man answered. The man on the line was Patricia's father, Benjamin Forrester, a rather stocky built man with balding hair. He had been on the town council for the last ten years getting reelected over and over. Before that, he had been a local pharmacist. When Joshua told him who he was, there was a pause and then a deep growl seemed to come from the speaker.

"Let me tell you something boy, you are never to see my daughter again. Is that clear? She was told that she could not attend the dance with you and then she does anyway. Then you go for a joy ride in the countryside and there is an altercation with my daughter in the car. Do you understand me boy? You are never to see my daughter again!" with that the line went dead and Joshua stood staring at the phone.

Patricia must have gotten into real trouble for lying to her parents about the dance and being with him. She must have told him about the incident on the back road. That really surprised him as she didn't want to talk about it. Maybe she thought her father could help with it. He would find a way to speak with her, maybe before school on Monday.

While waiting for his parents to come home Joshua went to his room and began to look-up incidents of nooses in trees on the web to see if there was any significance in his area.

Mr. Thomas Johnson called and said he had made arrangements for him to see Trinity Lance on Tuesday; three o'clock at the Pizza Place in the village. Joshua told him he would be there and was excited about it. Then he lay down to take a nap as his head was swimming with all the events of the last two days.

Chapter 28

At seven o'clock Josh was awakened by his parents. He had been in a deep sleep and was startled to find them standing over his bed.

"Joshua, wake up." his mother said. "We need to talk with you about something."

"Okay, I'm awake. What is it, is something wrong?" he said as he dragged his body from the bed.

"Let's go into the kitchen, we have heard some stories and want to verify them with you," his father said.

Joshua was a little nervous wondering if they were talking about the events of the night before. He threw his jeans on and headed for the kitchen where he found his parents waiting patiently at the kitchen table.

"Sit down son, we need to talk." His father seemed nervous and gestured for Joshua to sit.

"Last night you were a little late coming home." This was a statement and not a question and Josh thought perhaps it was just going to be his mother wanting to talk with him about his disobeying his curfew.

"Yes mom, some of the players went to a restaurant for something to eat before coming home and time got away from us." He had told his father this story and it was essentially true so he thought that should be the end of it, and he wanted to stay on track.

"You may very well have done that son," said his father, "But we heard that you attended the dance with Patricia Forrester. Her father had said she could not attend with you, and then you went for a ride on a back road and had some kind of situation. Can you tell us what happened?" There was a concern in his voice as he asked Joshua to explain.

"Wow news sure travels fast. How does everyone know about that already?" Josh was amazed that Patricia's parents knew, and his parents knew. Who was the one divulging the information so fast he wondered?

"Patricia said her parents were having a party and that instead of picking her up, I should meet her at the dance and that is what we did. Some guys at the dance said there was a party at the Drinker House; you know that party house outside of town? Everyone was invited so we thought we would just drive out there and check it out and then come home. The guys from the team were coming so we thought it would be fine. Everyone was going to meet there. On the way, Patricia saw something in a tree that freaked her out and wanted to go home so we turned around and headed back. Then we saw the guys and all decided to go for something to eat." He didn't want to say noose, he wasn't sure how to process this yet. Even though Pops had said to tell them, he wasn't sure he was ready for this conversation and his parents coming at him with the information took him by surprise.

"Aren't you leaving something out Josh?" his mother said, "The part about some guys threatening you?" She seemed to be visibly disturbed.

"It wasn't any big deal. A couple guys were trying to throw their weight around and act stupid. We talked to them, and they left." He was hoping she would buy this story instead of the truth.

"Mr. Forrester called and he was really upset. He said you took his daughter to a place that put her in danger and that you weren't to see her again. He used some pretty foul language for a town councilman. What do you make of that Joshua?" His father looked concerned, and Josh was getting mad just thinking about the way Mr. Forrester had spoken to him and then having the nerve to call his parents and speak to them in an angry manner.

"He had no right to do that dad. When I called to see how Patricia was, he told me the same thing. I would not have put Patricia in harm's way. We made a decision to turn around when we thought it didn't feel right. Who does he think he is calling and yelling at you like that?" Joshua was getting mad; this whole situation was being blown out of proportion, or was it. That noose in the tree was a large part of why they were getting out of the area last night.

"We think this could be a racial issue Joshua, and maybe we should have had this conversation before. We have never really discussed it because we never saw it as a problem before now." His mother was being sincere and he could see that she was really worried about what happened or what she perceived to have happened.

"Maybe it was mom, there were some looks of disapproval at the dance when Patricia and I were dancing, but we both ignored it. Then when we were invited to the Drinker House party, I have gotta say Patricia wasn't sure about going but I said let's just go and see. We can leave if we don't like it. Then on the way Patricia saw something in the woods that freaked her out and we turned around." He still wasn't sure he wanted to say it was a noose.

"What did she see in the woods son?" His dad was pushing. He knew there was more to the story than Joshua was telling.

"She saw a noose." Joshua said finally getting it out.

The look on their faces told it all. There were shock, fear and outright disgust.

"You saw a noose?" his mother asked.

"Yes Mom, a noose, but I didn't think a lot of it at first. Then the headlights of a car were coming our way and Patricia started freaking out. We turned around to get out of there. The football team was coming, and we stopped and told them we were leaving and the other car with the guys showed up and the team backed them down. They left and we went to the restaurant, end of story." He wasn't going to tell them about kissing Patricia, which was too personal and private and not part of the story they seemed concerned with anyway.

"This is very serious Joshua. Do you understand the implications of what a noose in a tree meant for you?" his mother said with a touch of anger in her voice.

"Yeah I guess I do but there wasn't any harm done okay. I think we should just forget it." He really didn't want to make this big a deal out of a night that he had wanted to be so special in other ways.

"We will have to think about this Joshua. It is a big deal, especially for you, even if you don't see it." His father said pondering the future of what he thought should be done.

"Well while we are at it I want to tell you something else." He knew this was as good a time as any to tell them about meeting Mr. Thomas Johnson and having a meeting with Trinity Lance. "I found a guy on line, a black man who helps young black men know who they are." He really didn't know quite how to explain Mr. Johnson or really how to tell them so he just said it.

"You found a guy online? Oh Joshua what are you doing? This could be dangerous for you. You have no idea who people you find online are or what they could do to you." Joshua could see this conversation was not going in the direction he planned when agreeing with Mr. Johnson to tell them.

"No, you don't understand. I met him and he is a nice man. He helps people know who they are, sorta like a preacher." He wasn't sure how that sounded either but he was on a roll and had to get it out.

"This is not good son. You went and met with this man. Where did you meet him?" his father said.

"I went to the city, met him in a restaurant where there were others around. He is a nice man. He has made arrangements for me to speak with a lady right here in town next Tuesday." He wasn't sure how that information was going to play out.

"You have what?" his mother said.

"Yes, she's a social worker or something like that. She's a black lady and Mr. Johnson thought my talking to her might give me some of the information I've been looking for." He reached in his jeans pocket and produced the card Thomas Johnson had given him.

"What kind of information are you looking for son?" His mother looked really frustrated. "What do you want to know from some stranger? Why haven't you asked us about whatever it is you want to know?"

"Look Mom, I love you both, you know that. But there is something missing in me. It has nothing to do with my feelings for you. My being black and your being white, I just don't think you understand how I feel sometimes. Seems like everything around me is white and I am trying to fit into a square peg while I am round. The people I am talking to are black. They understand. I am thinking this lady, Trinity Lance, can give me some insights, that's all there is to it." Then he handed the card to his mother.

When Joshua said Trinity Lance and his mother saw the card with her name on it, the color drained from her face. She got up from the table and walked to the kitchen sink. It had finally come full circle. She knew the birth families name was Lance and she knew that he had a sister. They had never told Joshua about his family. They wanted to keep him protected from the past of poverty, brokenness and shame. At that moment she questioned all of those decisions. He had the right to know who he was and where he came from. Her concerns were selfish. She was afraid he wouldn't love her as his mother and that is all she had ever wanted in her life was to have a child that loved her. Joshua's father got up and walked to the sink and put his arms around his wife.

"Nancy, I think it is time to tell Joshua the truth about his family. He needs to know. You can see that can't you?" He was being gentle and compassionate. He knew how adopting Joshua had changed her life and made her feel fulfilled. This, however, was about Joshua and his feelings, and he felt it only right to tell him the truth.

"Yes, you are right." She came back to the table and sat down, took Joshua's hand and began the story of when he was born and how she had first seen him after his mother had died. He had been brought to the hospital where she was a nurse in the emergency room at the time, and she had immediately fallen in love with him. He had been put into social services care and they petitioned to adopt him. He had three siblings; two brothers and a sister. They knew the siblings were teenagers at the time and never connected with them or really knew what had happened to them. His birth family's name was Lance.

When Joshua heard the name Lance, he looked shocked. That was the name of the lady Mr. Johnson had set up the appointment with for

Tuesday. Could it be possible that the lady was going to be his sister? He could see this was hard on his mother. At the same time, the thought that he could possibly meet someone of his birth family was exhilarating. He got up from the table and paced the kitchen trying to take it all in.

"Why haven't you told me any of this before?" he said, looking at his parents.

"We just didn't want to confuse you, or that is what we thought. We would give you the best life we could and love you with all our heart. We thought that would be enough." His mother was in tears now. She felt so fragile and was afraid he was going to hate her for keeping this secret all his life.

"Mom, I know you love me and I have had a good life. That is what Mr. Johnson reminded me of. He said that God had protected me and put me in a safe place and that I had a destiny to fulfill. I'm not mad at you Mom. I love you." With that he went to the table and put his arms around his mother to reassure her that he was going to be okay and that this information was just that, information that he could use to help him move forward with his life. His mother collapsed into his arms and continued to say she was sorry.

"Do you want us to go with you to meet this Trinity Lance?" His mother was hoping he would say yes, but was sure he would say no.

"No Mom, I have to do this on my own. I'm a big boy now, and I have to do this alone."

His mother made dinner, and they ate together. Joshua said it had been a long two days and he was going to bed early. He wanted to process all he had learned from the time he went to see Thomas Johnson to telling his parents how he felt. Then there was that prayer he had said with Mr. Johnson and the possibility of meeting someone from his birth family. He decided to pray, after all that is what Mr. Johnson had said would change things. Just look at all the changes that had happened since he said that prayer with Mr. Johnson.

Chapter 29

The heavens were full of excitement. The battle had been brewing for days, ever since Joshua Lance Hardgrave had asked Jesus into his life. The fallen were plotting and scheming trying to figure ways to get Joshua to sin and walk away from the commitment he made to have Jesus help him with his life. The fallen hated these decisions. It only made their lives harder, and the righteous were always interfering with their plans, stopping them at every turn. There must be a way to tempt this young man and get him to renounce his decisions. Money didn't seem to affect his decisions; his life was comfortable. He was at the age where sexual hormones would be raging. Perhaps that was the best avenue to take. Then there was always Mr. Benjamin Forrester getting involved, and they could take down two enemies at one time. They laughed an evil sort of laugh that gurgled from their throat as they began to plan how they would chart the events of the next few days.

Joshua began to pray. "God I am not good at this, in fact I don't really know how to pray but Mr. Johnson said to just talk to you like you were a friend or like I would be talking to my father, only don't try to hide anything because you already know it, so here goes. So much has happened in the last few days, and I can see your hand has been in it. I want to thank you for helping us the other night when those guys were going to do us some harm. Thank you that I didn't get to know what that noose in the woods was for. Thank you for the guys from the football team coming at the right time and being there; they are like brothers. I believe Patricia is in trouble with her family. Could you help her with that? Most of all God, thank you for letting me find Thomas Johnson and encouraging me to talk to my parents. Thank you for the possibility of finding someone who might be my sister. Amen."

It felt good to pray. He pledged to do it more often. With that all said Joshua was so exhilarated and his mind so full of the event of the last few days he couldn't possibly fall asleep. He began to wonder what his sister might look like; would she know that he might be her brother; where could this go from here, and then he was asleep.

Joshua's prayer brought Ahlai to attention. He had his sword in a sheath that looked to be four feet in length; he was always prepared for battle being a warrior angel for the righteous. He was an angel to be reckoned with if anyone got into his way while on assignment. Ahlai would take Joshua's prayer directly to the throne room, then his master could intercede on his behalf. Ahlai would then receive his orders for the next assignment. He unfurled his wings and began a spinning motion that took him straight up and into the heavens. He would be sure to see Rafael on his way and give him the latest report.

Chapter 30

In Iraq, the last battalion was heading back to the base. It was the last tour of the day when the vehicle hit a land mine and everyone was thrown from the vehicle. Jeremiah Lance lay beside the road bleeding from shrapnel to his leg. When he regained consciousness, he looked to see if his men were alright. He could see Sergeant Billing's arm was missing and he was bleeding profusely. He yelled for a medic but there wasn't anyone to hear him. He reached for his radio to call for help. "Send a medic and get us out of here. We are all hurt, land mine." He was straining to hold consciousness; he was bleeding from his right leg. He grabbed his neck scarf and made a tourniquet, he crawled to his Sergeant and tried to stop the bleeding. 'How do you stop the bleeding when your whole arm is blown off', he thought. The other two men were beginning to come around. He yelled for someone to get on the radio; get help, take cover, and for them to get out of the open.

Within minutes help arrived and Sergeant Billings was hooked up to an IV. They looked at Jeremiah's leg and said they would get him back to camp and get the shrapnel out. One of his men, Joe Cummings from Lansing, Michigan who was only eighteen years old was dead; this was his first tour of duty.

After the medics got everyone in their vehicle, and the place was secured they rushed back to the camp hospital.

Jeremiah knew this would be his last tour of duty. This injury would send him home. Home he thought, 'where will that be? Maybe it is time to find my family.' This experience made him realize life was way too short and too precious to not have someone who would remember him. His deeds in life hadn't been too bad and maybe his life experiences could help make others stronger. With that he drifted off into a drugged sleep.

Chapter 31

Patricia was home alone. Her parents had gone to a rally of some sort. She was grounded and had been given a good tongue lashing by her father. She was forbidden from seeing or even speaking to Joshua. She felt there was more to the ordeal of the night at the dance than met the eye. Why was her father so furious with her? It wasn't like this was the first time she and Joshua had been somewhere together. They had known one another all their school life. She knew her parents didn't like the fact that he was of another race, but this was a new decade and people didn't act like that anymore. She decided to do a search to see if she could find out the whys. She went to her parent's bed room, and feeling extremely guilty, she opened her father's dresser. The first drawer held socks, underwear, nothing unusual. The second drawer had T-shirts neatly folded in rows according to colors. The bottom drawer however, held something that made her take a step backward. There was a sheet covering the clothing in the bottom draw. She lifted the sheet and there under it was a hood and a sash with a red symbol of the KKK. It said the White Knights of the Klan. There was a rope belt and some papers that said something about a Grand Wizard and the name Forrester on it. She was in shock. How could she live in this family all these years and not know that her own father was one of those bigots, one of those who put on a sheet and a hood and went out and did despicable things to other people, people of color? It was as if a light bulb turned on. Things began making sense; the night she heard her father use the N word and the late night meetings he was always attending. Did her mother know this? Of course she must. But how come I didn't know? she thought. Was that noose in the tree last night for Joshua, and did her father have anything to do with it? She slammed the drawer shut and ran from the room. She had to get out of this house. She had to see Joshua. She had to scream, cry, do something to make sense of this awful knowledge she just acquired. She ran out the front door letting it slam behind her. She ran until she couldn't run anymore and finally, found herself in front of Joshua's house. She began to process the information she just found. Suddenly she realized she didn't know how to tell Joshua that her own father was to blame for that noose in the woods. It was the only way he would have known it was there. She was barely home from the dance and he already knew. How could she tell anyone that her father was a monster, that he had been responsible for this despicable act of hatred? Joshua's house was dark so she decided to leave, walk, and think things out, and try to make sense of her life. She would be leaving for college soon. She would leave this area, and leave her parents' house. She would make a life of her own with her own values and her own beliefs. How could she look her father in the eye again and ever trust him? She had walked several blocks when, there in the dark recesses of the night was something lurking in the shadows. Patricia caught a glimpse of something. She felt fear and the hair on the back of her neck stood up. She had been so engrossed in her thoughts that she hadn't given any thought to where she was or how late at night it was. She started to back away and cross the street, but she knew there was something, or someone following her. She didn't have her cell phone. Her father had confiscated it so she couldn't call Joshua. She didn't have any money. She had left the house so fast, she hadn't taken anything. Her instincts told her to run. There wasn't anybody on the street. The way she was running looked darker than where she had come from but she had made the commitment to go that way. Panic began to well up within her. She thought to scream, but who would hear here?

The fallen had been patrolling the dark alleyways and haunts of the night when they saw Patricia Forrester. They decided to follow here, inflict fear on her, and maybe get her to run right into the drug boys they had been harassing all night. The fallen had been plying them with temptations of drugs, sex, stealing and evil. Once they gave into the temptation of drugs, it was easy to get them to do evil acts.

Patricia was in a full run with panic close to the surface. Why had she been so foolish? She knew better than to be in this neighborhood at night. It was known for drugs, prostitution and every other kind of hellish act.

Rafael had returned to his post. He had been listening to the prayer of Joshua Lance Hardgrave. Joshua had asked that Patricia Forrester be helped. She was going to be in a situation that needed some super-human attention. From Rafael's vantage point, he could see the fallen chasing Patricia. He saw the three men who were on the street in the alley ahead doing drugs. The men were drunk, stoned and wild when they heard her come. At first they thought it might be the police. They were known to patrol the area as it was a drug haven for the addicted. When they saw it was a girl running, the fallen began to whisper evil thoughts into the men's ears. "Go get her, you can have your way with her, she's a virgin." one of the fallen whispered.

"One of the men said, "Let's get her." They came out of the alley just as she was reaching the opening. Patricia stopped in her tracks, began to backup and catch her breath.

"Hi honey, what you doing out here at this time of night?" one of the men slurred.

She didn't answer. She was looking around to see if there might be a way to escape.

"Well you came just in time. We are having a party, and we needed some other guests. We got some good stuff for you to try," the shortest of the three said. His hair was dirty and his teeth were rotten. He slurred when he spoke.

"I'm not interested, thank you. I just need to get home." She was trying to hold her composure and decide which way she needed to run.

"Awe come on honey, you can party with us. You look like such a sweet young thing," the shaggy haired man said as he moved closer to her.

"No, get away from me!" she shouted.

"Feisty little thing," one said to the other as he reached to grab her arm.

Patricia took off running. The three men were chasing after her when from across the street came the headlights of a car. The police had been staking out the area for drug dealers and prostitution when they saw the young girl run toward the alley. They thought she was a prostitute so they didn't stop her but continued to observe until they saw she was trying to get away from the men in the alley. The three men stopped chasing and began to run in three different directions when they saw the police cruiser.

As she rounded the corner, Patricia saw someone leaning against a building under a streetlight. He was tall with broad shoulders; muscular by all accounts. He had long black hair tied back into a ponytail. She could see at once he was incredible good looking. He had a ruddy complexion and his eyes were bright emerald green and they seemed to bore into her. He wore cutoff jeans, a T-shirt and sandals. He seemed innocent enough and nothing like what she had been running from. As she approached he smiled and his teeth were so white they seemed to give off a gleam of light.

"Hi Patricia, what are you doing in this neighborhood?" he said as he stood up with his hands across his chest.

"How do you know my name?" she asked with a sly glance in his direction.

"Oh, I have known you for a long time." he said with a smile.

"From where have you known me? I would have remembered you if I had met you before." She stopped and waited to see if he was going to make any moves toward her as she continued to listen for sounds of anyone else following her.

"I knew you parents and met you when you were a young child. I have seen you at school also. Guess I didn't think you would give me another look," he said with a grin that seemed to indicate he was playing with her.

"Well I don't know if I would either." She began to move closer to him, cautious. She still wasn't sure what he wanted or who he was or why he was in this neighborhood.

"Do you go to school around here?" She was trying to make conversation to keep from panicking. She couldn't tell his age, maybe college-age she thought.

"You might say that." He moved from his place on the wall and took a step toward her.

"Well I know I have never seen you. I would have remembered." She had a sense of excitement while in his presence and an unexplained chill ran down her back.

As he approached, her impression was right. He was extremely handsome. She couldn't put her finger on it, but she had the feeling he was powerful; almost god-like she thought. She had a sense she had seen him before.

He put his hand out for her to take. As she began to reach for it, she heard something that scared her, and she froze in place. A flash lit the sky with such force that she fled into his arms.

"What was that?" she said in a terrified voice.

He began to laugh and reached around her. "That was just the god's playing games."

Again another flash and a peel of thunder roared. The skies opened up with rain in a torrential downpour.

"We need to get out of here," he said and put his arm tighter around her waist. They began to run. He was holding her with such force that her feet barely touched the ground. She had the feeling they were flying. Just as they rounded the corner, they ran full speed into someone. Her rescuer flung her around with such force; she let out a scream as she landed directly behind him.

"Well look who we have here?" the tall, dark haired, god-like rescuer said.

"What are you doing here?" Rafael asked.

"I seem to be rescuing this damsel-in-distress." he said with a smile.

"You know what I mean Ramiel." He glanced at Patricia with a concerned look on his face.

"Are you okay young lady?" the stranger asked.

This guy is huge she thought; broad shoulders, abs like a wrestler and he must be at least seven feet tall. He, too, was god-like she thought only in a different way. His hair was golden, pulled back, his eyes were brilliant blue. His hands looked powerful, like they were used to holding something heavy. The thing she noticed the most was his expression. It held concern, but another quality, something softer like gentleness.

"Raf, you know I am only following the rules, helping the unsuspecting who are heirs of salvation." He said with a sneer.

"You lost that responsibility long ago when you left your first place of importance." He said with such sadness in his voice it made Ramiel flinch.

"Excuse me gentlemen," Patricia said. She didn't really want to get involved in their disagreement; evidently they knew one another and were at odds with one another. If they began to fight, she didn't know which would win. They were huge. She found them interesting but at the same time disturbing. Also, of more importance to her at the moment, she was standing soaking wet in an electrical storm, even if she was being covered by two huge god-like figures.

The two men turned and looked at her. She was soaking wet, hair getting matted and her clothes dripping. "I believe I need to be going home, if you will excuse me?" She moved away just in time to see a police cruiser coming her way.

'Oh great,' she thought 'now the cops are going to be involved and my father is really going to kill me.'

When the rescuers saw the approaching vehicle they both turned and left with such speed she couldn't believe her eyes. "What in the heck was that all about?" she said to no one in particular. "Guess they are more afraid of the cops than the storm." She couldn't figure out where they could have disappeared to so quickly or more importantly who they were and how they knew her name. One had said Ramiel and he called the other Raf so she knew their names anyway. She would look into it another day, but right now she was going to have to explain to these officers why she was in this neighborhood soaking wet with no identification on her.

When the two angels reached the first heaven, they turned and addressed one another.

"You know the rules Ramiel." said Rafael "You are not supposed to engage with humans. It is forbidden in your state." Rafael was indignant.

"Hey look Raf, she needed watching over and I thought I would just drop in and see what I could do. I know this is an important case you are working on and since we are old friends I thought I would help." He was still smiling that irritating smile he always used in the past when they were working on something important together.

"She is not on your radar and you are not to engage. I do not need your assistance. You continually like to break the rules. That is why you fell." They had been the best of friends in the early years of their work together when the Father had placed them on assignments to watch over special cases. Then Ramiel began listening to the revolt, began hanging out with those who did not want to follow the law, or more importantly listen to the master.

"Have you ever thought of speaking to the Father? He might relent and allow you entrance back into the kingdom." He wanted Ramiel to be back to the place of power and dignity that had been his so long ago.

"I have freedom that you don't know about Raf. It is far more interesting with the leader than you can imagine, why don't you consider coming down and checking it out for yourself?" He knew Rafael would never leave his command. He had worked up to a position of great honor with the master and was trusted in all aspects of his service.

"You are foolish to think this will end well Ramiel. One day we will be on opposite sides in battle, and I believe you will be greatly overpowered when that time comes. Stay out of my affairs with this assignment. I will not have you, of all angels, getting in my business. He said this with such force that the thunder that roared over the heads of the humans below made them look to the sky to see what was taking place.

"We will meet another day Rafael," said Ramiel as his wings spread to full appendage and he ascended high into the atmosphere with one blast of air. He spun in a circular motion, then flew straight to the western sky with such force that the wind blew the trees on the earth.

"Yes my old friend, we will meet again and I am afraid it will be a battle with swords to the end." He lifted off with his wing span spread to the fullness of majestic grace and headed in the direction to where his charge would need his watching.

Patricia was crying now with fear letting way to relief when she saw it was the police. Also tears might soften the policemen's attitude towards her she thought.

"What on earth are you doing out here in this neighborhood at this time of night. Don't you know how dangerous it is?" one of the officers said.

Through tears and catching her breath she said, "I was out taking a walk, thinking about some things and I didn't even realize the time or the neighborhood. Thank you so much for coming. I don't know what those men would have done had they caught me." They seemed to be listening intently, not treating her like a criminal which made her more at ease.

"I'm not sure what they would have done either. What is your name and where do you live?" the officer said.

"My name is Patricia Forrester and I live on Blake Street. My father is Benjamin Forrester, the City Councilman, and he is going to kill me when he finds out where you found me." She didn't want to tell them who she was but she knew she had no recourse but to be honest. She didn't want to go home, but she had no other place to go.

"Mr. Forrester is probably going to be very upset that you are here, that's for sure. Get in. We'll give you a ride home. You need to remember what could have happened to you if we hadn't been staking out the neighborhood. It could have been very bad for you. Do you understand that young lady?" Officer Evans said in a stern voice.

"Yes sir, I do. Do we have to tell my father where you picked me up?" She was trying to figure out how she was going to get out of this mess along with the one the night before. Her father was going to be so mad. This was the part of town he was always talking about, saying it should be burned down and the trash gotten rid of once and for all. 'Of course.' she thought. 'Now I know exactly what you meant by trash.' Patricia guessed she would just have to deal with the details as they became knowledge. The two officers took her home and the house was quiet. She guessed her parents hadn't returned from the rally they attended so she thanked the officers and went into the house and to her room. Then she did something she hadn't done in a long time. She knelt beside her bed and prayed.

"God, if you are there, I want to thank you for protecting me tonight and ask you to help me sort all this mess out with my father and Joshua. Show me what I should do?" With that done, she dressed for bed and fell asleep immediately, from all the stress of the last few days and the exercise she had gotten from running tonight. Then she began to dream. She hadn't had this dream in years. It was when she was around four or five, and she was lost in the woods. Her parents had gone on vacation and a tall, dark haired man had rescued her and taken her back to where her parents were frantically looking for her. She woke up with a start and sat straight up in bed. "Now I know where I saw him before. He rescued me when I was a child." she said. "How could I have ever forgotten him?" She lay back down and thought about him. He looked the same she thought. He was dressed different but definitely the same person, or was he a person or a god? As she thought about this, she tried to go back to sleep.

Ahlai, one of the angels in Rafael's command had been watching the view in the alley. He had been put on assignment to watch Patricia. He had alerted the attention of the officers by a flash of light to the alley where Patricia had been running. The officers noticed a young girl running towards the alley. Ahlai knew that when they became involved, Patricia would be rescued and taken home where she would be safe. He had missed Ramiel who had made himself invisible standing in the shadows. Ahlai would have been really concerned if he had seen him. He was a higher ranking angel even if he was a fallen one, and he would not want to engage him in conflict.

Officer Evans, a short, stocky man, with balding dirty blonde hair, and in his late thirties had been on the police force for two years. He knew where Mr. Forrester was. He was at the meeting he couldn't make tonight because of work. They belonged to the same organization. Officer Evans called him after dropping Patricia at home and gave him the details of the night. Mr. Forrester thanked him and said he had done a good job, then went back to the rally to end the meeting with a prayer.

The fallen angels liked these kinds of meetings; they always fostered hate and violence and made for approval by their head master. There was always something in them regarding keeping the blood line pure and eradicating the blacks, Jews and homosexuals and anything else that didn't amount to their white supremacy ideas. The fallen were dancing with glee clanging their spears and shouting victory to our most glorious leader.

Chapter 32

Breckenville had been founded in the eighteen seventies by white farmers. The farmers used black labor to harvest their crops. It was a pro slavery town and in the nineteen hundreds, a mob had lynched two black men. Some of the oldest town folk remembered the time and dismissed it as "the hanging times". The town had been working for years to dispel their history. People went to church, stopped at the local restaurant for breakfast, did family things and sometimes the local teens went to the mall in the next town to hang out. Sunday was a usually quiet day for the town of Breckenville. This particular Sunday was going to be different. Word had spread that a noose had been hung from a tree near the Drinker House and the local NAACP had gotten wind of it and formed a rally to march on the city square. The city square had a tree that years past a black man had been hung on. Their signs included STOP THE HATE, BRECKENVILLE STILL BROKEN, NO NOOSES IN OUR TREES. They had called the local newspaper and the syndicated press in the next closest city. At ten o'clock it was all to start. A phone call was made to the Hardgrave home suggesting they come to the rally. A phone call was made to Benjamin Forrester the city councilman telling him a group of blacks were forming at the city hall and were there any specific instructions he wanted done dealing with this group?

Joshua's parent's decided that they needed to do something.

"Joshua, we need to tell you something. A phone call just came saying a rally is forming at the city square. It is about the noose that had been hung in the tree, and they want us to come." His father was a little disturbed by the connection they were making with his son and this situation.

"Where is this information coming from? How does everybody know about this? I don't want to go. This is getting blown way out of proportion" Joshua was not happy about being the center of this controversy and wished the whole night had never happened and wanted it to go away.

"Son, I think we should be there. This was directed at you, and it was sending a message that blacks better stay in their place. This is not acceptable. There are good people in this community that don't think like that. I, for one, am appalled that there are still some of those hateful people right here where we live. We will go with you to make sure that you are safe."

Joshua was weighing his emotions with his thoughts. He had never had to make a stand for who he was before. He went on about his life being black in a white world and had gotten along alright with most everyone he had met. He was a good student and on the football team. He would leave for college in the fall, and he had loving parents. Tuesday he was going to meet someone that might be his birth-family. This, however, might be bigger than all of those things.

"Okay dad, I'll go, but I am not going to stand up and make a speech or let anyone use me for their own ends. I'll go get ready. We'll miss church you know?" For some reason this morning he really wanted to attend church. It had just seemed important to him all of a sudden. With that said he went to his room to get dressed. 'What does one wear to a racial rally' he thought, one that he is the center of. His cell phone rang and he saw that it was Patricia.

"Hi Patty, how are you? I tried to call you but your father told me I wasn't allowed to see you anymore. You must have gotten into some real trouble. What's up?" He was wondering if he should tell her about the rally or just let her find out later.

"Listen, I heard my dad talking to somebody on the phone and he told my mom that some people were going to be meeting at the court house for a rally of some kind. I think it has something to do with the dance and that noose in the tree." Her father had actually said the N word but she would never use such a word and especially not with Joshua.

"Yeah, I know. We got a phone call too. They want me to come down and support it I guess. Some blacks protesting that noose hanging in the tree. How on earth do all these people know this? Your dad knows, my parents know, now the whole town is going to know, I think they are making more of it than it is, don't you?"

"You know what Joshua; I am beginning to believe this is a big deal. I can't believe there is still this kind of hate in the world, say anything about right here in our little town. I want to come too." She had made a quick decision, not thinking about what kind of collateral damage this would cause her at home.

"I don't think that would be a good idea Patricia. After all your dad was steamed at the idea of you and I going to a dance together. I'm not sure what he would think of you spending time at a rally for something like this. He read me the riot act about having you in a place of danger the other night. Who knows what kind of situation this could put you in?"

"I don't care! I'm part of this; after all it was probably because I was with you at the dance. I have a right to stand up for what I believe in, and I believe in you. It doesn't make any difference to me that you are of another race." She was determined now more than ever to figure a way to get out and be at that rally. "I'll see you there, and this has nothing to do with you as much as it does with me and my beliefs." With that she hung up and began to get dressed when her father called her to come to the kitchen.

"Patricia, your mother and I have decided that you need to go and spend some time at your grandmothers. We have been disappointed with your actions lately. You disobeyed a direct order not to attend the dance with that boy, and I understand you were out walking around in a very bad part of town last night. If it hadn't been for the police, you could have been seriously hurt. Your mother will take you there today so go and get your bags packed." It was a statement and there wasn't any room for disagreement, but Patricia was going to try.

"I didn't disobey you. I met Joshua at the dance just like a lot of other girls met guys. It probably wasn't the best idea to go for a ride to the Drinker House but there were a lot of others going as well, and we weren't going to do anything bad. Last night was a mistake. I went out running and before I realized it I was in the wrong end of town. It had gotten dark. There wasn't any intention on my part to do anything wrong. I think you are making way too much of this and trying to send me away." She was crying now and pleading to be able to stay.

"No young lady, it just shows your judgments aren't sound. A little time away will give you time too reflect on what it means to be part of a family and follow the family rules." He wasn't going to budge on this issue. There was going to be some turmoil in the town, and it was over this Hardgrave boy whom he knew his daughter was much too infatuated with. She needed to be away so he didn't get pulled into it politically as well as legally.

"I won't go! You can't make me! And I'm not sure I want to follow the beliefs of this family; they stink." With that she stormed out the front door and headed for the court house at a run.

Benjamin Forrester grabbed the phone and called the local police department. "Officer Evans, I need you to intercept my daughter and make sure she doesn't go to the court house. She is walking or running in that direction." He was not going to have his daughter's picture in the paper with a bunch of blacks. He didn't want it perceived that she was supporting their cause.

"Yes sir Mr. Forrester, I'll get right on it." After he hung up the phone he told his fellow officers, "That guy needs to get a reign on this kid of his or she is going to cause him some real stink. Let's go see if we can locate her." Then they got in their cruisers and headed for the court house.

Patricia was running just like the night before only this time she could see where she was going, and she wasn't going to let anything get in her way. She headed across Glen Avenue to Howard Street then to the Veterans Park. She took all the back streets and then through the park, she didn't think she would be seen by her father or the police if they tried to intercept her. She reached the court house where there were a hundred blacks forming around the tree in front of the court house. Their signs were being held for the camera men to see and hopefully get on the nightly news. She didn't see Joshua and found herself a little self-conscious being the only white person in the group. A couple of girls came up to her and asked what she was doing there.

"I'm meeting a friend here, Joshua Hardgrave. He's a friend of mine." When she said Joshua's name they knew she must be the white girl he was with when they saw the noose.

"I think there are some people over there that would like to talk with you." They said pointing to the center of the group.

"I think I will wait here until Joshua comes," she said, not wanting to be the center of attention in a sea of black. She began to feel the way Joshua must feel at school or at functions when he is the only black among everyone white.

"Well suit yourself. I know they would be interested in what you have to say," said the one girl with dreads in her hair and making a sort of snickering sound, as she left to go towards the center of the group where the organizers were.

Patricia noticed a police car coming in the direction of the court house from South Main and decided she didn't want them to see her since that Officer Evans didn't keep his word about telling her father about the night before. She decided she didn't trust him. She instinctively headed toward the steps of the courthouse. There were columns she could hide behind and still see all the proceedings that were going on. She should be able to see Joshua when he arrived too.

Chapter 33

The rally was well organized for being put together at the last minute. It had only been twenty four hours since the event had taken place. The news media arrived at nine forty five and Joshua and his parents arrived at ten. The local police and the county sheriff's office had twenty officers to keep the peace. The local black church had a choir standing on the steps of the courthouse; singing "We Shall Overcome". They were peaceful and orderly. When Joshua and his parents arrived, someone ushered them to a platform. Joshua wasn't sure he liked the idea of being put in the center for everyone to see him. He didn't see Patricia but had a feeling she would be there if at all possible. She should be easy to find as all the faces he saw there were black except for his mother and father.

A man who looked like some kind of preacher began to speak.

"Ladies and gentlemen, we are here today because there has been an injustice in our community." Everyone began saying "yes, yes."

"A young man of color was threatened with a symbol of hatred and injustice. This cannot be tolerated in this day and age." Everyone was saying, "Amen, Amen."

"This young man was going about his business, going to a dance, having some fun with his friends and someone, someone with hate in his heart, was leaving him a message that he has no right to be in this community."

Joshua was becoming uncomfortable. They were talking about him, and he hadn't come to that conclusion at all, or at least not until this moment. Was someone really trying to tell him not to be there?

"This young man was at a dance with a white girl. In fact, everybody there was white except this young man. He later was taking a ride with this white girl, something he has every right in this United States of America to do in this year of our Lord. However, those who still hold prejudice and segregation in their hearts made a decision for this couple that it was not right. They decided for them that they had no right to be together."

Patricia was becoming nervous. She knew they were talking about her and Joshua. She knew that her father was going to be furious. Having his daughter's name in the paper and on the news tied to a race issue would affect him politically. She knew what his feelings about this issue were since finding the clothing in his dresser. It was too late now. She was here, and she could see Joshua was here, sitting right in the front row. She wondered if he planned on saying anything, and mentioning her by name. Should she go and stand by him, and let the whole world know where she stood. Let her father deal with his hate issues himself. There was a lot at stake: her college tuition her parents would be paying for, her name in the community, her family. She had to make the right decision. What was it her father said about the family rules and knowing when to stand with the family?

Just when the speaker was about to point out Joshua, a parade of cars came down the street. They parked a block away and out emerged twenty people dressed in sheets and hoods and carrying signs saying, "KEEP IT PURE", "KEEP IT CLEAN". They marched double file down the street right up to the court house. The police held back the crowds and allowed them to march. The black choir began to sing again and some people in the front began to yell "Go home! We have a right to be here."

From where Patricia stood she could see the whole street. Nothing was out of hand, yet. She could feel the tension from the crowd. People were now shouting back and forth. She was looking for Joshua and his parents. Joshua turned to his mother and father and said, "Let's get out of here. This is turning into something I never bargained for." They turned to leave when one of the black men leading the rally grabbed Joshua by the arm and said into the microphone, "This man has every right to be here. He doesn't deserve a noose." With that, everyone turned toward Joshua, who was visibly shaken by the fact that he had been thrown into the front lines.

Everyone began to yell "Every right!" Joshua pulled away and started down the steps toward the sidewalk that led to their parked car.

A newscaster made his way toward Joshua and stuck a microphone in his face and asked "How do you feel about the noose in the tree and do you plan to sue anyone over it? Who was the white girl you were with?"

Joshua pushed the microphone away, and with his parents, pushed his way through the crowd. The men in sheets where having verbal exchanges with the group of black men and the police were beginning to surround the groups to keep them separated. Patricia could see that Joshua was leaving and wondered how she could leave her vantage point to get to him without the news media seeing her and knowing she was the one with him that night. She eased her way down the steps and across the court yard. If she circled around the courthouse and crossed the back parking lot she could make it down the street and catch the Hardgrave's before they reached their car. She made a run for it when something very unusual happened, the sky opened up and it began to rain. It was a torrential rain, with thunder and lightning. Patricia took off running. Everyone began looking for some place to take cover under. The police began giving orders to disband. The Hardgrave's reached the car just as the rain started. Patricia reached them as they were starting the car's engine. She knocked on the car window. She was getting soaked, and Joshua opened the door and let her in.

"What on earth are you doing here Patricia?" Mrs. Hardgrave said.

"I heard about this meeting when I heard my father talking to someone on the phone. I knew it was about us last night and I thought I should be here to support Joshua." As she said the words, she was thinking 'even though I was hiding behind a column on the steps.'

"This turned out very badly," Mr. Hardgrave said. "I am disappointed that the Klan showed up. Who knew they were still active in our little community? I am not sure how this is going to play out in the newspapers and on the evening news. I think you both should stay very low-key for a while." He was definitely concerned about them as a couple and since the Klan was involved it could be even more dangerous for his son as well as Patricia. Who knew the Klan and prejudice existed in their community?

"My parents are sending me away to my grandmother in Tennessee," Patricia said. "My dad thinks I have been making some bad decisions lately. I think he is more worried about his own reputation as a politician in the community." She knew she probably shouldn't have said that last part but she was still upset by what she had found in her father's room.

"Your grandmother, when is this happening?" Joshua was stunned. They only had a few weeks left of school. "What about exams and graduation?"

"I don't know. My dad can probably fix it with the school and I can take my exams at my grandmother's. Who knows if my father will let me return to graduate here?" She hadn't thought about this and after today she didn't know if he would ever let her come back here to be with her school classmates, say anything about seeing Joshua again.

Chapter 34

The heavens had been in preparation for battle for days.

The chaplain's prayer group and the local churches had been alerted to an altercation of some sort and had been watching and praying for their town and their county. They had started before the dance and several in the group had felt the call to continue in prayer through the weekend.

The righteous angels were an orderly group, led by command, and always on guard for evil plots. The fallen, on the other hand, were ready but not as orderly. They were always in disagreement as to who was going to lead the charge or who was going to be the strongest, evilest or vilest. They had their orders from a higher ranking upward but they always quarreled amongst themselves when their commanders were absent.

Everything was geared for a Sunday morning confrontation at the Breckenville County Court House. Since the churches held services on Sundays, there was always righteous on hand to do battle against evil. Today however, they would be given orders to protect a group of people who had come together to proclaim justice and righteousness. This infuriated the fallen. The fallen would have their own kind on hand; those who didn't know the truth but had believed a lie of arrogance and pride. They would disrupt the group, and cause havoc; as they always thought they would reign supreme. This was another lie they believed.

The battle began in the heavens and spilled over into the streets of Breckenville. When the righteous were being victorious the heavens opened up with thunder, lightning and torrential rain. This caused the group on the streets to scatter and the righteous were sending the fallen squealing and whining back to the dark recesses of their abodes. There would be another day to do battle in the future, and the righteous would again win the battle as long as there were those who prayed.

Chapter 35

Trinity Lance had heard about the rally from the morning paper. She had been out of town for the weekend, or she would have been at the rally with some of her friends. However today she had more pressing matters to attend to. She had an important meeting this weekend. She saw a picture of Joshua Hardgrave and tried to see if there could be any family resemblance. She was more intrigued than ever now to meet him on Tuesday. She decided to do some family research before the meeting. The weekend had been extremely profitable; she had gone to the prison to meet Elisha.

Elisha had been excited about a visit from Trinity. Pops hadn't said it was his sister, but he only knew one Trinity and figured it had to be her. When Trinity had applied to come, she had to give her identification and stated she was Elisha's sister. She hadn't been to a prison before and was a little apprehensive about the process of entry. She had to go through a security system that scanned her for anything that could be contraband. She had to place her personal belongings in a locker. She could take some money to use in the canteen machines for coffee or snacks. She hadn't seen Elisha in many years and wondered if he was as handsome as she remembered him as a young boy. She always thought that was why her mother favored him so much because he was such a handsome boy.

Elisha's had become hardened over the years of incarceration but was still good looking. She was surprised by his broad shoulders and short hair, which he had cut years earlier after meeting Pop's Johnson. He had tattoos with wings that wrapped around his arms. His smile was broad with white teeth that were straight and even and gave him a smile that was pleasing. The hardness could be seen in his attitude and walk more than in his physical appearance. When she got to the visitation area, she spotted him immediately. The family resemblance was still there and something inside of her leaped at the thought of seeing a family member after all these years.

Elisha got up but stayed at his place as instructed by the corrections officer. She came to his table and sat down just looking at him for a long time.

"Elisha, I can't believe it's you. It has been so long since we have seen one another and so much has happened in our lives. Are you well?" She had thought of what she was going to say when she saw him but all those speeches were gone when she saw him face to face.

"You look incredible," Elisha said as he took her hand.

"So do you. I can't believe I am here with you." She was shaking from the emotions of the moment.

"I can't believe how you found me here and how you met with Pops and that you actually came." Elisha was finding it hard to say the words that were welling up within him. It had been so long since seeing family. He had been praying lately for just this meeting. He knew he would be leaving prison in a few months, and didn't know what he was going to do. He knew Pops would help him on the outside, but he was really scared as to how he was going to make it after so many years of incarceration.

"I believe this is a God-thing Elisha. Meeting Pops was just the beginning of putting things in place. Did he tell you about Joshua?"

"Joshua?" he said with a little astonishment. "No, he never said anything about a Joshua. Is that your boyfriend's name?"

"No, but wait until I tell you. I had to go and visit a client that was working at a restaurant in the city. I got there at noon and there weren't any seats left. I asked this man to sit with me, he looked friendly and non-threatening."

"That must have been Pops." Elisha said.

"Yes, exactly, it was Pops. Anyway, we talked, and he told me this story about a young man that he had been in prison with and our last

watched

names were the same. Can you believe this?" She was getting excited just thinking about that meeting. Elisha was also getting excited. He knew Pops prayed a lot and didn't believe in coincidences so he believed this was all orchestrated by God Himself.

"So after all of that Pops said he had met a young black boy by the name of Joshua. He thought that if I could talk with him it could help him. This young black boy was raised by a white family and is in his teens and really searching for who he is and where he was supposed to fit. Of course I couldn't help but think about our baby brother. I know he was adopted, but I never looked into it. I know I should have, but so much drama was going on when we were teens and mama died. I just went to live with Trish and went to school and vowed to get out of our old lifestyle." She bowed her head and took a deep breath.

"I guess that meant forgetting about Jeremiah and me also?" Elisha had thought about this before, and it just came out. It didn't have as much malice as he had carried over the years of thinking about it. Seeing her sitting here talking to him face to face had softened those years of disappointment.

"Yes I guess that is true. I just didn't know what to do about you. You were so angry about mama dying and social services taking us and splitting us up. All I knew to do was try to survive." Trinity had tears streaming down her cheeks. There had been so many years of emotions pent up inside of her.

"Hey, it's okay. We all survived with what we had to do. It wasn't your fault I ended up going to detention and then to prison. I made that choice that day myself. I was so mad at what had happened to mama, and the gang just seemed to be my family. When that kid said something about mama, I just exploded. I damn near killed him, and if those other guys hadn't pulled me off, I would have. I was an angry boy and became an angry man until I met Pops. He just showed me how to be a man without all the anger. He told me about God and showed me by example. He watched over me while he was here and taught me how to defend myself without having to fight everybody. I owe him a lot." Elisha now had tears in his eyes. This was something he didn't do in front of anyone; especially in this place anyway. That was a sign of weakness. He wiped his eyes with his arm and leaned across the table; he placed a hand on Trinity's and said, "This is the best day of my life, you coming here to see me. It is an answer to some prayers that I have been praying for a long time."

Trinity was so moved by this statement that she wanted to reach across the table and take him up in her arms and hug him. When she reached toward him, the officer on duty blew a whistle and told her to stay on her side of the table. She sunk back down and with longing reached for his hands and held them tight.

"Elisha, I am going to meet Joshua on Tuesday, and I don't know what it will mean but I am going to try and get our family back together. I have some access to records as a social service employee. If this is our brother, I am sure he is going to want to know about you as well as Jeremiah. Do you know anything about where Jeremiah is or have you ever heard from him?"

Elisha was interested in getting the family together. This would give him some purpose to look forward to when he got out. "No, I never knew what happened to him. Maybe Pops can help you with that also." He had a lot of confidence in Pops, or in God using him to bring about miracles.

"I know he went into the service. I think it was the Marines. If that is so, I think I can look up some records and find out where he is. Let's pray that God will bring him to us and we can make our family whole again." With that they lowered their head and held hands and began to pray right there in the middle of visitation with all the other people around talking, laughing and having their visit.

"God we know that you have brought us together today, and we give thanks for that. We now humbly ask that you might bring the rest of our family together. Joshua and Jeremiah are out there somewhere, and we would like to see them. We ask this in your name. Amen."

They raised their heads and laughed at the thought of all the noise and chatter going on around them and how it had been blocked out for a few moments of prayer. They continued their visit sharing how Trinity had gotten her job and how Pops had been an influence on Elisha and that he would soon be getting out and needing a place to stay. Then their time came to an end.

The fallen watchers over the prison were in a tirade. This was a place they hung out a lot; influencing to do evil. To have prayer going on during their temptation time, during visitation, was making them rankle. The fallen would try to entice inmates with sexual arousals during visitation. They tried to get visitors to bring in contraband and to get anyone they could into trouble. When the prayers began, they had no choice but to stand back. The righteous would come and remind them that they had no place in prayer- time and they were not to interfere.

"This is our place. What right do you have to be here?" said one of the more aggressive fallen.

"There are many who serve the king and you know the rules. When two are together praying in His name, you must stand back," the righteous said with strong conviction for the rules.

"We are aware of the rules, but rules are not what will stop us from our assignments today," one of the smaller fallen squealed.

"This may be so, but as long as we are in attendance, you will remain far from our charges. Is this understood? We will drive you all the way back to hell if you disobey." The righteous were standing with swords drawn and looking very much in charge.

These smaller fallen ones whined and snickered but moved to the corner of the room near the ceiling and cringed at the sight of the righteous angels with their swords drawn ready for attack.

Chapter 36

Patricia had packed her bags before she had headed for the rally. She decided that going to her grandmother might help her figure out why her parents believed the way they did. She had not spoken to either of her parents since the night before. The Hardgrave's had wanted to take her home, and they offered to speak with her parents about the matter of the past events. Patricia knew that it would be a scene and did not want to subject Joshua or the Hardgrave's to her father's wrath. She said if they could drop her off on the corner she would walk the rest of the way. She was wet and tired from the rally. When she entered the house she could tell her father was furious. He was waiting in the living room for her.

"Who do you think you are?" he said with controlled anger. His face showed signs of strain, and perspiration was beading on his forehead.

"I think I am a friend, and friends stand by one another." She knew this was dangerous territory for her to enter but she said it anyway.

"Friends you say. What about family and standing by family values?" He was almost shouting and moving towards her. He continued to rant about obedience and her disrespect for him and her mother and that she was never going to see that boy again. She tuned them out and simply went to her room making her father even angrier.

"She has to leave today, do you understand?" He spoke to his wife, the walls, and the very air to declare his wishes.

"I will make arrangements for her to go to my mothers. She hasn't seen her for a while, and mother would love to have her there," Patricia's mother said.

"I'm not sure that is the best place for her." He was calming down now and realizing that his daughter had her own thoughts and his demanding was not winning the battle. "She needs to be in a safe place where they can't find her." He said this with a touch of concern she hadn't seen in some time.

"She will be fine, and I can drive her there later today. Stay for a few days and return in a week or so."

The matter was settled and they left around four to get there by late in the evening or early morning of day three.

Chapter 37

William Hardgrave was surprised in Benjamin Forrester's reactions to all of the events of the past weekend. He was city councilman and had been re-elected over and over for the past several years. The whole racial issue was something he thought Forrester would have used to get more publicity for himself. He wasn't anywhere near the rally, at least he didn't see him there. Forrester's reaction to his daughter and Joshua being seen together at the dance and riding in a car together had made no sense to him. They had worked on committees together over the years, and he had heard him make remarks that didn't seem appropriate, but he never thought Forrester was a racist. He thought perhaps it was because he had been contemplating running for office himself and maybe Forrester had gotten wind of it and was afraid he might lose his coveted position on the town council. William decided he was going to look into the matter a lot closer come Monday; maybe call the party affiliates and get his name on the ballot for the coming election. The Mayoral race was coming up; maybe he should try for that. 'I think it's time for a change in Breckenville; 'maybe we need to fix some of the things that are broken,' he thought before going to his office to check on some records regarding Joshua's adoption.

Chapter 38

As soon as Benjamin Forrester knew his daughter was out of harm's way he made a call to Tom Sullivan of the Federal Bureau of Investigations.

"This is Benjamin Forrester I need to speak with Agent Sullivan. It is regarding a very important matter," he told the receptionist that answered the phone.

"Just one moment Mr. Forrester, I will connect you." she said with a pleasing voice.

"This is Tom Sullivan. What can I do for you Ben? I didn't expect to hear from you for a week or so." He was surprised that Forrester had contacted him so soon. They had planned on a meeting the following month to finalize all the plans for the upcoming events.

"Well, things have developed, and we need to talk. Did you see the news of the events that took place down here?" He was sure he must have seen the coverage. It had been on all the stations in the area.

"Yes I did. What the heck is going on down there? I thought you had things under control." He knew it was a hot bed in the area. They had kept an eye on these radical groups for some time and having someone on the inside gave them the leverage they needed and the information to eventually shut their operations down.

"Well things have changed. That girl they were talking about, the white girl."

"That wasn't your daughter was it? Incredible of all the girls this kid could have picked, he has to pick your daughter."

"Yes it was, and when my family becomes involved it is time for me to step back. I am not going to put my daughter in danger. She already thinks I am some kind of monster and bigot." He was getting agitated just thinking about the events he was about to uncover.

"We can keep your family safe, you know that. Do you want me to send an agent down there to keep your family under protection?" He didn't want to do that, it could cause suspicion and they were so close to closing this case he didn't want to blow it now.

"No, I have sent her to her grandmother's in Tennessee. I believe she will be fine there. She still doesn't' know anything that is going on. There will be a time to let her know, but right now I am only concerned with her safety." He was sure Thomas Sullivan of the FBI could understand his situation. They had spent many hours together planning this undercover operation and talked about family and values. He was a family man himself. Had two sons who were in college and said he would do anything for them.

"What do you think we should do?" Sullivan said.

"I think I need to talk with William Hardgrave. He is a decent man, a lawyer in town, and he is the father of the black boy that was targeted. I think he would be a good person to have on our side." He had thought about this all night and came to the conclusion that William Hardgrave could be more of a problem than a help if he didn't understand what was happening.

"I don't know Ben. This could be tricky; him being the father of the boy and all. It is obvious that he isn't a racist since he and his wife adopted this boy. Does he have a strong sense of community?" Sullivan had to be sure this was going to work before he signed off on anyone else being aware of their operation. To take down the group that had set up shop in this little town had been his ambition for some time. The group was found to be a front for running guns and ammunition to other organizations in the country. They had all the making of a terrorist organization. Benjamin Forrester had agreed to infiltrate the group under the guises of being a member of the Klan. He had helped the FBI with a case when he was a young man just exiting college. Because his name was the same as the late Forrester who had first formed a group of Klansmen during the Civil War, he could use that as leverage. He had no ties to the original Forrester family or to any Klan involvement but found himself interested to the point he agreed to help when the FBI contacted him. He did some snooping around, led a small local group to believe he was a cousin to the great Robert Forrester and that his belonging to the group could give them clout with the other groups. It had worked. He had retrieved information that brought a man who was suspected of murder to justice. One of the members had killed a man in a bar fight and tried to cover it up. His Klan brothers buried the body and all pledged to an oath of secrecy. When Forrester discovered the secret and the place where the man had been buried, he notified the FBI who told him to get out of the group and move to a new location. They found the body, arrested the men involved, and closed the case. Forrester went on to meet a girl, fell in love, and moved to Breckenville and eventually ran for political office. It had been years since he had heard from the FBI, but one day he got a call. Someone wanted to meet with him. Ben thought it was in regards to the old case, so he went. They had another case in his own town and since he was so respected it wouldn't be suspicious if he became involved using his old alias. He took several months and discussions with his wife before agreeing to the terms. When they found what they needed he would be moved to a new location. His daughter would be going off to college, and they wouldn't have a lot of ties to the area so if they would relocate them he would agree to the covert operation. Now that Patricia was involved, he wasn't sure it had been the right decision.

"Meet with Hardgrave, feel him out, and see if he is willing to go along with our plans. If he is, we can move this operation up. I think we have enough information. You can set up a rally either at the location of the group headquarters or a location they all would feel comfortable attending. Actually this new event can play into our hand. They should all be willing to come and collaborate against a common enemy. When you have the time and place set up contact me. We will have the area surrounded and take this group down once and for all. With the new Home Land Security terrorist rulings, we have more resources and will be able to put these guys away for good. You're doing a great job Ben. Keep up the good work." With that they said goodbye and hung up.

Ben Forrester immediately got on the phone and called William Hardgrave. He had to get things worked out before his family got hurt.

He answered the phone, "Bill Hardgrave here." He had been monitoring all the calls since the incident and the events at the courthouse. They had been harassed by the media and every other group of nuts out there who wanted to talk to Joshua or just wanted to make crank calls. When he saw it was Ben Forrester calling, he wanted to speak with him and he answered immediately.

"Bill, this is Ben Forrester. Can we get together and talk? I have something I want to share with you and can't do it over the phone." His voice was sincere and strong.

"I think that would be a great idea. I have a lot of questions about what has been going on and don't think I have all the answers yet. When and where would you like to meet?" This was a surprise call, one he welcomed more than any he had had received in the last few day.

"How about the Silverbrier Country Club? They have a good lunch menu. It shouldn't be too crowded on a Monday and we shouldn't be bothered by reporters as it is an exclusive club." Ben had tried to think of a place that wouldn't draw attention to them after the news had splashed their picture all over the paper with Joshua. 'White folk and Black Son', the headline had read. The article went on to tell the Hardgrave story about adopting Joshua and sending him to an exclusive school like Somerset.

"That would be fine. I have a ten o'clock appointment but should have it finished by eleven. I can meet you at eleven thirty. If you get there first, I will find you. I want to thank you Ben. I think we need to talk." He was sincere about that. He had always thought him a decent man but there always seemed something mysterious about him.

"That will work for me. I'll meet you at eleven thirty in the club house. See you there." With that done, Ben Forrester set out to make arrangements for a rally to be held at the Drinker House. That should be a good place; out of town, close to the members' property. All parties should be willing to come and then he would notify Thomas Sullivan. He would go to Tennessee and get his family, move them to a new location, send his daughter to college and be done forever working undercover with the FBI.

Chapter 39

"Wow, did you see that coming?" Ramiel said to Azrael.

Azrael was an angel of death. He had an air of superiority about him. He was one of the larger angels, dark brown skin, weaved black hair and eyes dark as deep pools of water. All angels respected him. He was always roaming the outskirts of heaven making sure everything was done in a timely manner. When it was time to take someone to the next destination, he made sure it was done swiftly and on time. His orders were to be followed to the minutest detail by those under his command, and he never allowed insubordination.

"There are always unexpected events we are not always privy to when it comes to the humans. They were given the freedom of choice and we can never be sure just what that choice will be. Sometimes we can surmise by the actions they take but again at any moment, they can change their mind when another choice presents itself." Azrail had been a wise angel, had seen many things over the eons and so he was never surprised when he saw a change happen.

"You would do well not to get so involved in the affairs of humans. You lost that privilege long ago. You know what needs to be done. Perhaps you need to think more on that." With that said Azrail mounted up and spread his wings. He moved with grace and agility and was gone before Ramiel could even reply.

Ramiel had been patrolling the area of the Forrester homestead. He had been curious as to what had happened with Patricia after she had gotten home the night the police intercepted his rescue.

"There are strange events taking place. Seems the enemy and the victim are collaborating. I wonder what it all means." The angels had insight into human affairs but did not have access to their will and the choices they made. Sometime the only thing they could do was stand by and watch, and if they could deduct what kind of plans were being made, they could then try to intervene and cause havoc on their situations or create situations that could help the humans make wiser choices.

Rafael had also been observing at the Hardgrave home and heard the conversation regarding a meeting with Benjamin Forrester. He made a mental note that this should have a patrol around their meeting to keep them safe. No prayer had been incited for them to move, but he would order a battalion to be at the country club and would make it a point to go and see Ramiel. If something was about to happen with the Forrester family, he knew Ramiel would be involved. Ramiel had taken on the Forrester family when Patricia was born, some sort of vindication of when he had lost a charge before he had fallen. He had rescued Patricia Forrester in the past and he was there the other night to make sure she was safe again. Rafael wasn't sure what Ramiel was up to but he wasn't going to give him a chance to intervene in the plans that were about to be made available. The Father had given him information about the future, and he had to handle it very carefully. He could not interfere with the human's choices but he would guard and could create a diversion when needed. 'If only Ramiel would prove himself to the Father,' he thought. 'I believe the Father would forgive and allow him back into the regiment.' He had always been a good and loyal comrade until that time he lost his charge and had gotten angry and cursed all of heaven. 'Even angels need forgiveness,' he thought.

Chapter 40

Jeremiah had been sent to Bethesda Naval hospital to have treatment on his leg and physical therapy. This had given him time to think on what he was going to do with his life outside the military. His whole adult life had been centered on being a Marine, and now he was going to be a civilian. The idea of being a civilian was unnerving to him. He didn't know where any of his family was, he had never taken a wife; he didn't think it appropriate to leave a wife and family at home when he might get killed in battle. Most of his relationships were with other Marines; men he trained with, did battle alongside, saw injured and die. The United State Marine Corp was his whole life and now it would be gone. Well 'Sempra Fi' he said to himself.

There was one thing he had made a decision on while in Iraq. He would find his family and see how they were doing.

The nurse came into his room, "How you doing today Lieutenant? Are you in any pain?"

Pain was something he had learned to deal with over the years. However the pain in his leg was a constant throbbing. The medicine would relieve the pain, so he had welcomed the medicine they were giving him.

"I could sure use something to stop that throbbing in my leg. Is that ever going to go away?" he said to the nurse as she came with a syringe filled with liquid relief.

"With some therapy and a little help from my friend here in the needle, you'll get through this. You're a tough guy Lieutenant Lance. I have faith that you'll have this behind you, and you'll be out dancing and romancing in no time." With that said she stuck a needle in his leg, smiled broadly and left his room.

Nurse Brenda Harper was a petite brunette with a broad smile and a happy disposition. She was a Marine nurse who had been at Bethesda for five years working as a therapeutic nurse to those returning home from battle. She had chosen her field because of compassion and the loss of her own brother during a tour of duty in Iraq. Jeremiah thought he could get to like her. There was something about her that made him comfortable. He determined he was going to get to know her better but right now he was going to let this liquid gold take its affect so he could sleep awhile before they came to get him for therapy.

Jeremiah's guarding angel was standing by his bed, strong and regal looking. His shoulders were muscular, and he stood seven feet tall. He wore a white robe that was cinched at the waist with a gold braid and attached was a gold sword. Jeremiah didn't know he was there but had a sense that someone was near and that it was okay to give into the medicine and sleep. The watcher was being vigilant to see that none of the fallen came by while the medicine was taking affect. There were fallen that liked to menace when people were on any kind of medication that could alter their emotions. The fallen could see the guardian on duty and pass by his room to go to others who were cursing God for their pain and nightmares from war. Jeremiah drifted off to sleep and thanked God for the relief.

Chapter 41

Joshua could hardly wait for Tuesday to arrive. He had dressed three times trying to think of which would make the best impression when he met Ms. Trinity. He settled on khaki shorts, a polo shirt and Nike sneakers. He was more nervous than he thought he would be. He left the house an hour early to make sure he was there in plenty of time and found it only took him fifteen minutes to drive to The Pizza Place. He waited in the car for ten minutes, then got out and paced the parking lot.

Trinity pulled into the parking lot a few minutes before their meeting time. She wore white slacks with an orange and yellow blouse and sandal heels. Joshua spotted her immediately and thought she looked absolutely beautiful. He slowly walked up to her.

"Hi I'm Joshua Hardgrave and you must be Trinity Lance?" he said stronger than he thought he would be able to speak.

She smiled a broad smile that showed perfect white teeth. "I am, and I have been waiting to meet you ever since Mr. Thomas Johnson told me about you."

"He is quite a guy, and I think it is pretty amazing how he met you and me and now we are meeting one another." He had taken her hand and felt an immediate connection.

They entered The Pizza Place and found a booth toward the back. There were only two other customers in the restaurant at the time, and they were engrossed in conversation and didn't even look their way when they walked past.

Trinity began carefully, she didn't know how much this young man knew about his past, and she didn't want to scare him off.

"Joshua, how much do you know about your family?" she said.

"The Hardgrave's or my birth parents?" he asked cautiously.

"Well both, I guess. You must know a lot about your Hardgrave family, as I understand; you have been with them from birth." She wanted him to reveal as much as he knew before she gave him pertinent information.

"Mr. & Mrs. Hardgrave are really good people. They took me in when my mother died and gave me their name. I go to a private school although it's a white school and as you can see I'm not. They have made sure I have the best of most things. I am leaving for college in the fall. I have had a pretty good life considering my beginnings I guess." He said this with consideration for the only parents he had ever known and the fact that he cared for them as if they were his real parents. They were the only ones he knew.

"It sounds like you have done well." She smiled and reached for her handbag to retrieve some pictures she had brought with her.

"I want you to see something. These are pictures of my family when we were all younger. I have three brothers although I am missing a picture of the youngest." She handed the photos to him and sat back to see what his reaction would be. She noticed right away the resemblance he had with her other two brothers. He took the photos and began to inspect the faces. After several minutes he raised his eyes to hers and said "they all look familiar somehow but I know I have never met them, have I?" He handed the photos back.

"No, I don't think you have or at least to your knowledge. The oldest is Jeremiah, and he is in the military. I am looking for him as we speak. He went into the Marines shortly after our mother died. Elisha is the middle brother, and sad to say, he is in prison soon to be released. In fact, I went to visit him for the first time in many years at the prison last week, and I was pleasantly surprised to see he had turned out so well considering he had spent so many years incarcerated. He was a really angry boy after our mother died, and he joined a gang. He got into a fight and nearly killed a boy who had harassed him. He has paid with many years of his own life for that one angry outburst." She was watching his face to see how he was processing the information she was giving him. He seemed to be taking it all in with eager enthusiasm to learn more.

"What happened to your mother and youngest brother?" He was almost holding his breath with anticipation of the answer. He had caught the fact that their mother had died and believed this could be the answer he had been long waiting for. His mother and father had told him about the Lance family after he had confessed meeting Mr. Johnson. He was hoping for confirmation from this woman, who could possibly be his sister.

"Our mother died giving birth to our youngest brother." she said.

"What happened to him?" He could hardly breathe. His throat was going dry, and he was on the verge of grabbing Trinity and shaking her for more information.

"He was adopted by a white family and his name is Joshua." She hardly got the words out when he dropped his head and began to cry. The anticipation of this moment had played across his mind over and over. Now, he was hearing it from his own sister. He had noticed immediately that the boys in the photos looked a lot like him when they were his age, and he knew the moment he met Trinity that they were connected somehow.

Trinity got up and went around the table and slid in next to him. She put her arm around him. She was finding it hard to find the words for this special moment. Joshua looked up into her face and smiled. "You have no idea what this means to me. I have family; family that looks like me, is the same color that I am, someone who can tell me what my real mother and father are like." He put his arms around her and held her tight. The other people in the restaurant didn't seem to notice or even care that this monumental moment in time was happening right in their presence. A few minutes later she returned to her side of the booth and the waitress came to take their order. They ordered pizza and drinks and settled in to begin filling in the blanks of Joshua's life.

"So Elisha is the same guy who was in prison with Pops?" Joshua asked in amazement.

"Yes and it seems all the pieces of the puzzle have been coming together with Pops being part of the picture," she said.

"What happened to my mother?" Joshua asked. "She died giving birth to me. Am I to blame for her death?" This thought had never occurred to him before this meeting. Had he somehow been to blame for his mothers passing?

"She was having complications and didn't want to go to the hospital; didn't want to spend the money. Our father had left, and we didn't have much money so she was doing things on her own. She went into labor and the only one around at the time was her friend Trish whom she called to come and help. By the time Trish got there, she was already in big trouble. By the time the ambulance arrived, she had given birth but they couldn't save her life. She had written down that you were to be called Joshua, and I guess the adoptive parents honored that. You weren't to blame for mama's death. She just wasn't in good health. She just never took good of care of herself. She was always thinking of us kids, and daddy was a mean man who only showed up when he needed something. Mama finally told him to leave us alone. I guess when she died, he didn't want the responsibility of raising four kids, and he never showed up again. I went to live with Trish and went on to college to get a degree and become a social worker. When I went on a case in the city I met Mr. Johnson, Pops and the rest is history. I saw your picture in the newspaper with that incident of the noose in the tree. I would have been at that rally, but I was out of town for the weekend visiting Elisha. You must tell me about that incident and what all happened." Their food was delivered and they looked at one another, Trinity said, "I think if there ever was an occasion to give thanks, this is it." They both bowed their heads.

"Thank you Father. You have brought us together and are blessing our lives. I thank you for bringing Joshua back into my life. Help us to mend the past separation that has taken place with all of us. We look forward to the day we can all be together as family. I pray this in Jesus name. Amen." They raised their heads and smiled. They both knew this was the beginning of a new era in all of their lives.

Joshua's attending angel, Rafael, was standing guard. He was the highest ranking righteous, and they all took orders from him. He had given orders to secure the area until the truth was announced. He told them to keep their places until given further orders.

"This is the day the Lord has made," Rafael said. He stretched his wings across the parking lot. He had been standing guard to the restaurant, not allowing anyone access while this moment was taking place.

"We have fulfilled our duty to watch over this family. They have come to the right decisions and found one another. They have had answer to prayers that had been sent to heaven." He stood with raised sword and shield to ward off any of the fallen that might be attempting to intervene in today's chosen destiny.

As the meeting inside The Pizza Palace unfolded, the guards relaxed their positions and by the time Joshua and Trinity were leaving, they had allowed others to enter the restaurant and dismissed some of the righteous to other duties.

Joshua headed for home wondering how he was going to explain all that had happened to his mother and father. He wondered how they would take the news that he wanted to go to a prison to meet his brother and was going to work with Trinity to find his brother Jeremiah. He decided to pray and ask for the right words to say so his parents wouldn't be hurt by the great news he had to share. He wondered about Patricia. He wanted to talk with her, but she had said something about going to visit her grandmother and that she would call him as soon as she got there. There was one other person he wanted to talk with and that was Thomas Johnson. He felt he owed this man a lot for putting all the pieces of his puzzle together. He was going to call him first thing and set up a get together, maybe even include his parents. He wanted to look up something on the computer about nooses and lynching's before going to see Mr. Johnson.

When Joshua arrived home, he went directly to his room. He turned on his computer and typed in lynching's in Florida. He accessed The Lynching Calendar and he counted three hundred and thirty six lynchings to date. One hundred and seventy were unidentified and they were all black. He found articles about local lynchings. He sat back in his chair. 'This is way more serious than I had thought.' he said to himself. 'Tomorrow I will talk with Mr. Johnson about this.'

Chapter 42

On Monday, the day before Joshua's meeting with his sister; William Hardgrave and Benjamin Forrester met at the Silverbrier Country Club. They were both on time and greeted one another with a hand shake and a cordial hello. They found a table in the corner trying to find some privacy.

"I can't tell you how pleased I am you called." William Hardgrave said. "I have wanted us to speak since the incident after the dance." He was sincere and concerned, as any father would be thought Ben Forrester.

"Yes I wanted to also William, but there are some other things involved that I need to share with you that will explain my actions of the last few days." He hoped and prayed this man was going to be his friend and keep his confidence.

"Call me Bill, Ben. I don't think we need to be formal."

The waiter came to the table and they ordered coffee and sandwiches and settled in to have a conversation. Ben Forrester explained about his past involvement with the FBI. He talked about how they had contacted him years ago to infiltrate the local Klan and get information about local groups that could have terrorist involvement and the possibility that they could be gun running along with other illicit affairs. Bill Hardgrave hung on every word he was saying. He was astonished, amazed and very interested in everything that was being said. Ben acknowledged that there was going to be a big raid on a meeting that he had arranged and it was to be within the next week. He also stated that the FBI was going to round up all those who participated in these activities and arrest them and charge them with terrorism and maybe even the Rico Act.

"Why are you telling all this to me Ben?" Bill wanted to know why he was privy to this kind of information.

"I want you to know so you will promise me, that if anything was to happen to me, you will make sure that Patricia is told the truth. If my wife tells her she will think she is just trying to make it out that I am a good guy, which I am but right now she doesn't believe that. I know if it came from you that she would believe it." Ben was being very honest and sincere. He had thought everything through and came to the conclusion that something could go wrong and if it did he wanted the true story to be told.

"I would be more than honored to do that, but do you think there could be some real danger to you?" He was now concerned about the information that had been given to him. He saw Ben Forrester now in a whole new light; a man of great courage and a man of deep conviction. He was not a bigot, a racist as he had thought the other day when all the commotion came about the noose and his daughter being with Joshua.

"What else can I do? Is there anything or any way that I can be of help?" He was sincere. This was going to be something really big for their area, and it made him wonder who could be involved in the community.

"There are some on the police force that are involved in these groups. Make sure that Joshua stays close to home for the next week, at least until this thing plays out. I have to be honest with you, the FBI decided to act now because they think the issue with Joshua and the noose would bring the groups together on a common cause. We don't want to see some crazy radical, racist go out and try to make a name for himself using Joshua as the pawn. You understand my meaning here don't you Bill?" He hated to tell a father that his son might have been used as bait to something so dangerous without their permission. He waited to see how Bill Hardgrave would respond to such a suggestion.

"I see how this would bring all those kinds of groups together, like minds and all. I must tell you that I am a little disturbed that it happened at all, and since you have come to me with the truth I believe we can be vigilant to keep Joshua on a short leash and watch that he doesn't enter any areas that could cause him harm. Thank you again for being so honest with me. I wish the best for you, and if there is anything else I can help with, please feel free to contact me."

"Well Bill, I will be leaving the political arena when this blows up." Ben said.

"I was considering running for mayor. Have you got any tips for me?"

"Yes. Be careful who you trust. After this, they are going to need some good men to run the town."

After lunch they left with a handshake and a promise that when this was all behind them, they would get together as families if at all possible.

Chapter 43

Rafael and Ramiel were in the atmosphere of the Silverbrier Country Club, not to either one's surprise. They decided to be on good terms, making small talk about the past, how the command had grown in the last few years, that the Father was always aware of what was happening, and that there were others who missed him in their company. It felt good just being friends, not engaging in debate over affairs that were not of their choosing.

"Remember one day we will be judged by our actions and those we have had charge over. They will know if we did all we could during our assignment. Perhaps you judge yourself too harshly Ramiel. You need to keep that in mind. Give it great consideration my friend. It may not always be as you see it. There are others who see it in a much different way. The truth is always the truth." With that, they departed the area.

Chapter 44

Trinity made the arrangements for Joshua to go to the prison with her and visit Elisha the following Friday. Joshua got permission from his parents to go as he didn't have any final exams that day. They arrived at ten o'clock. Joshua had never been to a jail, prison or anything that resembled one. Trinity had advised him not to bring anything that wasn't necessary as he would not be allowed to bring anything in. He would go through a metal detector; if anything set the detector off, he would be searched. He would be asked to remove his watch, jewelry, belt and shoes. He would be asked to empty his pockets. After going through the security procedure they would be led through gates and doors to a secure area. The doors would close and lock behind them. Joshua was going to make sure he listened intently as this was going to be such a new experience for him. They would be led to a visitation room. It would have several tables with chairs on both sides. Elisha would have to sit on one side, and them on the other. They would be able to shake hands but no other contact would be allowed. Occasionally a guard would allow them to hug on arriving or departing, but it was frowned upon. They would remain in their seats except to go to a canteen machine for a beverage or snack. There may also be children in attendance as some families come to visit.

    The security procedures went well and they were seated waiting for Elisha to come to their table. When Joshua saw Elisha he immediately saw the resemblance to himself. Elisha sat across from them and stared in disbelief. He too saw the resemblance with the exception of his tattoos. His eyes began to water and he lowered his head. Trinity reached across the table and took his hand. Joshua didn't know what to do, he sat in silence.

"This is a great day for me," Elisha said.

"It is a great day for all of us Elisha," Trinity said.

Joshua extended his hand across the table and said, "Hi Elisha. I am Joshua Hardgrave, and I believe I am your brother." He was smiling waiting to see what his new- found brother would do.

Elisha took his hand, leaned down and kissed it with tears dropping on them. "You do not know how much this means to me Joshua." He raised his head and smiled back at him.

They spent three hours talking, laughing and planning for the future. Elisha was scheduled for release in three weeks, and Trinity said she had made a place for him at her home. They would work on getting him acclimated to life on the outside. They would go and see Pops and thank him for all he had done helping to reunite their family. They retraced their steps to exit the prison and drove back to Breckenville feeling the day had been an extraordinary awaking experience.

Chapter 45

Jeremiah, in the meantime, had started a relationship with Nurse Brenda. His therapy had come a long way, and he was using a cane. He saw her every day for three months and now was seeing her in a non-patient relationship. She had been easy to talk with, and he had divulged his life story. She had been very sympathetic and offered to help him find his family. They had gone online looking for a Lance family in the area where he lived when growing up. He was sure some of them would be in the same area. They went on the Florida Prison Inmate list for information regarding Elisha. He was actually the easiest to find since his incarceration was there along with his crime and prison he was incarcerated in, it held his release date, just three weeks away. Brenda said she had time coming and she would drive him south to find his family. They left on the following Sunday and arrived in Florida two days later.

"This is going way beyond your call to duty, Nurse Brenda." He said as he pulled her close to him. She had really made an impression on his life. He would not be going back to Iraq, Afghanistan or any other war to fight and was now thinking a relationship would be what he needed. What better than to have your own personal nurse?

"This is my pleasure Lieutenant Lance, after all you are a superior officer and I have to follow orders now don't I?" Brenda had really fallen for this guy, maybe because she felt so alone herself. Her brother had died in Iraq, and he had been the only family she had left. Both of her parents had been killed in an automobile accident when they were young. They were raised by an aunt and uncle, but since they had children of their own, they always had felt to be second best in the family. She and her brother had decided when they were old enough, they would join the Navy and sail away or at least that was a young child's dream. She was glad she had joined the service, but at times, she had a longing to be part of someone or something that could make her feel needed and alive. Jeremiah Lance seemed to be just the thing she needed, and she was going to do whatever she could to help him become part of her life. They really seemed to have a lot in common when it came to their life stories.

When they arrived in Florida, they checked into a motel and called the prison to see if they could make arrangements to visit Elisha Lance. Jeremiah asked to speak with the warden and explained he was Elisha Lance's brother and had just returned from Iraq after being wounded. He hadn't seen his brother in many years. The Warden would make a special compensation for him if he could prove what he said to be true. Jeremiah said he could show his Marine credentials and his wounded leg. The Warden didn't believe that would not be necessary. On the next day he was entering the prison. Elisha was told he had a special visitor and since it was not his visitation day he didn't have a clue who it might be.

Jeremiah was not only given access to see his brother, the Warden also made arrangements for them to visit in his office. Since Elisha was a short-timer whom would be leaving the prison in a few weeks and had been a model prisoner, the Warden felt he could afford him this special treatment. When Elisha was ushered to the Warden's office, he was nervous that something might have happened regarding his release date. When he walked in the office and saw a Marine in uniform standing at attention, he couldn't believe his eyes. He stopped in his tracts and looked at the man in uniform and knew this had to be his brother Jeremiah. The moment was too much, and he collapsed on the floor to his knees with his hands on his face, tears dropping to the floor.

Jeremiah walked closer to him and said, "Look up soldier, be strong." When they were young children and their father would come home and inflict pain and suffering on the family, Jeremiah would say to his brother, "We are soldiers and we need to be strong."

Elisha got up and grabbed his brother around the neck and hugged him.

The Warden allowed them to visit for an hour giving them time to catch up and for Elisha to talk about Trinity's and Joshua's visit the weekend before. This had to be a miracle. Their whole family had come to together and Jeremiah was leaving the service as Elisha was leaving the prison. Jeremiah said he would see Trinity and Joshua and make arrangements to stay in the area for a time. He still had to be formally released from the Marines. This was the most amazing thing that had happened to him in years, and he had someone he would like everyone to meet, Nurse Brenda Harper.

Jeremiah left the prison, thanked the Warden, and headed for Breckenville. Next on the list was to find Trinity and meet Joshua Hardgrave, his long lost brother.

Breckenville hadn't changed. A few new stores had been added. The courthouse and the Main Street were the same. The population was seven thousand, two hundred and six, so the sign entering town said. There were two sides of town, the uptown where the whites lived and the other side of the tracks where most blacks lived. Jeremiah had Trinity's address from Elisha and headed for her house. To his surprise it was in the uptown area. It was the middle of the day so she would probably be working, but he wanted to see where she lived. Jeremiah and Brenda then found a motel, and stopped for lunch in a quaint restaurant on Main Street. They would make plans for a reunion. Brenda suggested buying flowers for Trinity but couldn't come up with an idea for a long lost brother. While seated in the restaurant, Jeremiah noticed a police officer in the back booth staring at them. 'Guess it isn't common to see a Marine in full dress' he thought, never imagining that it was because he was a black man with a white woman.

Jeremiah and Brenda were waiting for Trinity when she arrived home. She gave almost the same reaction that Elisha had of total elation. They had dinner together and spent the evening talking. Trinity wanted them to stay with her but they explained they had a motel room. They would get together tomorrow and make plans for a reunion of the whole family.

Chapter 46

They were standing at the perimeter of the Drinker House in the skies above. Rafael and his regiment were there to observe as the fallen had taken possession of the surrounding area. Ramiel was on the outskirts watching the proceedings. He had made the decision days before that after this night he would go to the Father and throw himself on the courts. He would admit that he had been wrong in leaving the kingdom; that he was sorry for his actions and beg to be reinstated in the Kings Army. He prayed that the Father would relent and allow him back into heaven. He had been beguiled by the leader's words. He had listened to his lies about a special truth that would bring them all enjoyment. All of the leader's words had been deception. Those fallen that had listened were now shrunk in size as they were not allowed into the light to keep them nourished. He had seen those who had been grand in size be reduced to sniveling imps under the leader's hand. If they disobeyed orders, they had their wings clipped and were no longer allowed to fly long distances. They were assigned to back streets and dungeons where people of depraved minds did their dirty deeds on earth. The leader still had those who were mighty with powers and were not to be reckoned with lightly. Only the righteous angels like Rafael could battle the fallen with those powers.

Rafael noticed Ramiel in the outskirts and wondered if he was going to be a challenge this night. Rafael decided when this night was over he was going to Ramiel to ask one more time for him to relent and leave the leader and come back to where he belonged. They were a mighty duo, and he missed his friend greatly.

"One more time my friend and then I will not be able to ask again," Rafael said as he ascended to a better vantage point to watch the proceedings of the rally that had been called by Ben Forrester.

Ben Forrester was to be observed. Rafael may even have to intercede although he had not received orders to do so. The fallen were in great numbers and sometimes made a covering you couldn't see through. He then made a decision that could cost him his rank but thought it had to be done. He went to Ramiel.

"Ramiel my friend, I am going to ask a great request of you." He said this with such sincerity that Ramiel gave his full attention, even though he had been enthralled by the proceeding below.

"I need you to keep an eye on these proceeding for me. I have to go to the Hardgrave home and make sure everything is as it should be." He wasn't sure that Ramiel would agree but he had to give him a chance to redeem himself. Rafael knew that Ramiels presence would not cause suspicion from the other fallen.

Ramiel wasn't sure what his old friend was asking. "What do you want me to do Rafael? Are you asking me to take your place here and observe and record the findings for the Father?"

"Yes, can you do that? We are not to intercede. We have not been given orders to do that. Can you do this for me?" He hoped that Ramiel would agree and this event would help to convince Ramiel when he spoke to him later upon his return.

Ramiel didn't hesitate as this would play into his plan of going to the Father. He could prove that he was a worthy angel and may even be granted forgiveness.

"Yes comrade I would be honored to stand watch for you. Go do what is needed. You can trust me to be obedient."

Those were the words he wanted to hear from Ramiel, and Rafael left praying that he would be wise and fulfill his duty.

Chapter 47

They began arriving at five o'clock for the rally that Ben Forrester had arranged.

'By six o'clock we should be able to start this rally. If I never see the likes of these people again, it won't be too soon,' thought Ben Forrester.

Officer Evans had arrived early to help with the arrangements for all the groups to have their own tables. He wanted this to be an orderly meeting, and he wanted to be noticed as a leader. His aspirations had been duly noted by members of all the groups. He had been a faithful follower that wanted nothing more than to be the next leader of the Klan or better yet an overseer of all the groups.

"Everything has been arranged. All the tables have been set, and we should be able to start on time." he said to Ben Forrester.

"You're doing a great job Evans. I think tonight you should lead this meeting. Give the opening address and tell everyone why we are here. You know the agenda so I think you should lead." Ben had wanted to give this over to Evans for some time and couldn't think of a better time than this so he could incriminate himself.

"Sounds good to me, we will start in five minutes." Evans was elated that he would lead this meeting especially with all the group involvement. It was just what he had been lusting for.

Ben had worn his robe but would disrobe after giving the signal. He knew the FBI would break upon the scene after he had excused himself to disrobe to his street clothes in the men's room. He didn't want to be caught wearing anything that would associate him with this group. When the FBI burst in, he did not want to be recognized as the leader. He had asked Officer Evans to take that honored distinction. Thomas Sullivan had assured him everyone knew who he was and he would not be harmed. Sullivan had said they would give everyone enough time to arrive, start the meeting and then they would enter; all he had to do was give the signal. All doors would be sealed, and no one would be allowed to leave. He would be arrested with the rest, handcuffed and taken to another location where he would then be whisked away to his family in Tennessee and then on to a new location. He would come back to testify at trial and sent back into the protection program. He was wearing a wire so they would know the exact timing. Forrester said he would excuse himself from the meeting go to the restroom and signal by saying "I'm finished." He had said that would be an appropriate phrase as that is exactly what he would be when this assignment was over. He would be finished with this group for good.

It seemed almost everyone had arrived close to the prescribed time. Any stragglers would be arrested down the road and held from getting to the meeting. Everyone was in high spirits and greeting one another and speculating the outcome of the night's events. There were some in robes and some in camouflage and some in black pants and shirts with insignias saying white power. Officer Evans called everyone to order and began by saying he was impressed with the attendance. He then began going over the events of the night of the dance and what had transpired, the protest at the court house, and an overview of what they needed to do now. He then opened the floor to ideas. After several verbal exchanges about killing and pillaging, Ben stood and took the floor. Evans sat down and grumbled under his breath.

"Comrades! To facilitate such a large scale event as you speak of, we would need to have a good size arsenal at our disposal." He knew the FBI would need this type of information in order to shut down these groups. He needed them to incriminate themselves.

"Is there anyone here tonight that can handle this part of the plan?" he asked.

Several hands went up in the back of the room.

"Can you identify yourself so we know who to give credit to and who to contact if someone needs to receive weapons?" He knew he was pushing for specifics, he knew the FBI would need this type of information. He hoped no one would be suspicious.

After giving their names and affiliations, Ben thanked them and turned the meeting back to Officer Evans and excused himself. After removing his robe and speaking the code phrase "I'm finished," the FBI began knocking down the doors.

Then Ben Forrester found himself face to face with Officer Evans.

"You know I have been suspicious of you ever since I saw you meeting with William Hardgrave at the Silverbrier Country Club. You didn't see me but I saw you. I was there to do an investigation of one of the cooks about a theft that had taken place, and low and behold, there you were having a cozy lunch with Hardgrave. Thinking how it was your daughter who was with that kid, I got to thinking something didn't smell right so I started watching you. Then tonight to turn the meeting over to me, now that was very unusual. Then I hear the doors breaking in and here you are all cozy and safe away from the activities going on in the other room." Officer Evans had extracted a small revolver from his left ankle. Everyone invited had been instructed not to bring fire arms to the meeting. Now Evans knew why. Ben Forrester didn't want any of the cops getting shot.

"Hold on Evans, this isn't like it looks." Having removed his robe and wearing regular street clothes didn't look good for him to Evans. No one would remove their symbol of commitment before a meeting was over.

"Just how does it look then Forrester?" He said with a growl. "Open your shirt." He said with the gun pointed directly at Ben's head.

"We need to get out of here Evans. What are you doing? Let's find a way out." He needed some time and thought perhaps he could convince him they could escape. Surly Sullivan would get to him before Evans used that gun.

"You know there isn't any way out of here, that is why you excused yourself and came in here. Now open your shirt." This time he cocked the gun and pointed it directly between Ben's eyes.

Ben began to unbutton his shirt when Evans grabbed the shirt and ripped it from his body. There it was, taped to his chest, an electronic bug. Evans had stepped back and leveled the gun to Ben's chest and pulled the trigger. Forrester was a traitor and if he was going down for his involvement, lose his job, go to jail then Forrester was going to die.

The place was a mad house. Everyone was trying to run but all the doors had been blocked. A few in attendances had weapons on them as they never went anywhere unprotected. Shots were fired and the FBI returned fire with accurate precision. Thomas Sullivan headed for the men's room to find Officer Evans gun in hand standing over Ben Forrester's bloody body.

"Drop your weapon." Sullivan ordered.

Evans turned slowly to look at Agent Sullivan, saw the FBI badge and gun drawn. Before Sullivan could respond Evans put the gun to his head and pulled the trigger.

"Get an ambulance here ASAP!" he called on his radio. He checked for a pulse on Officer Evans although he was sure Evans was dead. There wasn't any way he could be alive with the trajectory of the bullet to his head. Then he leaned over Forrester and checked for a pulse and found it was faint but at least it was there. He grabbed some paper towels from the counter and placed them on his chest. He knew this was a fatal wound; he was bleeding profusely. Ben opened his eyes and saw it was Agent Sullivan.

"You have to get to my family and keep them safe, tell them the truth. Promise me." He was barely audible.

"I promise. Just hang on. The ambulance is on the way." He wanted him to fight this one last injustice. This just wasn't the way it was supposed to go down. He was supposed to get out and take his family away, then to testify and see these people go to jail. The wound was too much and Benjamin Forrester gasped, closed his eyes, and died.

There were two angels that made their way to the men's room at The Drinker House. One was Azrail and one was Beliel. Each was going to usher a soul to his resting place. Azrail was taking Benjamin Forrester to a peaceful rest, and Beliel was taking Officer Evans to a place he never dreamed in his wildest dreams, a place he would find tormenting for all eternity.

Chapter 48

William and Nancy Hardgrave made arrangements to have a family reunion for Joshua. It was the least they could do. They had taken care of this young man since he was a baby, and now he had found his birth-family and they were going to make them part of their life as well. Joshua had assured his mother that she would always be considered his mother and that he loved her very much and appreciated all that she had given him. She had been able to accept that and decided the best way to show it was to have everyone come together. William Hardgrave said he knew the perfect date to have the reunion as Ben Forrester had said there was going to be a rally on Saturday and to make sure all the people he loved were where he knew they would be safe. This would make for the perfect time and place for the reunion.

Joshua had given Trinity's number to his mother, and Trinity arranged for her brother Jeremiah and his girlfriend Brenda to be there. Elisha, however, was not expected to be released from prison until the following week. William Hardgrave set out to see if he could pull some strings and get him released a week ahead of schedule. He knew the district attorney and the judge and he would call the warden if need be. Elisha had been a model prisoner over the last few years and since he had served his entire sentence with the exception of the first year without disciplinary reports, the judge agreed to vacate his sentence and he was allowed to be freed the Friday before the reunion. William Hardgrave would pick him up and deliver him to Thomas Johnson who had agreed to keep him a secret until the night of the reunion. Thomas Johnson would bring him to the house promptly at six o'clock.

Thomas Johnson was so elated at the events that had transpired that he could hardly contain himself. He was going to see Elisha again. The judge had been impressed with the story William Hardgrave had told him about his son Joshua and was glad to assist in the reunion given the bad publicity in the past weeks about the noose in the tree and the protest at city hall. Thomas Johnson couldn't believe how God used him to get all the right people in contact with one another, and Mr. William Hardgrave had insisted he be there for the reunion. He was going to get all dressed up to go to this special night, and he was going to see that Elisha had some proper clothing as well. Then he bowed his head and gave a prayer of thanks for all the wonder of it.

One other person Joshua would have liked at the reunion was Patricia Forrester. Joshua had tried several times to reach her. There was no answer at the Forrester home and when he called her on her cell phone or texted her, he didn't get any response. This concerned him. But he thought for sure she would get in touch with him soon. He had so much to share with her, and he knew she would be as elated as he was that he had found his family and his questions had been answered.

Chapter 49

Someone was knocking on the door and the phone was ringing. 'Who could it be at this time of morning?' Joshua thought. As he came from his room, heading for the door, his father stopped him.

"Don't answer that son."

"Why not and why isn't someone answering the phone?" Joshua was rubbing the sleep from his eyes.

"Come into the kitchen and get yourself something to eat or drink. We need to talk." his father said.

Nancy Hardgrave answered the phone. "No we have no comment." she left the receiver off the hook. "This is crazy. They have been calling for hours."

"Who has been calling for hours, what is happening?" Joshua asked.

"Last night there was a raid on the Drinker House and several people were arrested for criminal activity and Benjamin Forrester was killed." his father said.

"What? How could this happen, does Patricia know?" he stood up and went to the front window and peered out. There were news vans and people with cameras pointed at their house and people knocking on the door.

"Sit down son; I have to tell you something that Ben Forrester told me a couple days ago."

William Hardgrave began telling Joshua what Benjamin Forrester had told him. How he had been working undercover for the FBI. Mr. Forrester wanted Patricia to know the truth and that he intimated that something might go wrong. He was concerned for your and Patricia's safety after the night of the dance, and the noose in the tree. He decided something had to be done immediately, before anyone got hurt. Thomas Sullivan from the FBI called me early this morning to tell me. He said that they were going to put Ben's family in a protection program and we wouldn't be able to reach them. He would tell Patricia the truth about her father.

After a night of great joy for finding his family, Joshua was now crushed to hear about Benjamin Forrester and the possibility of never seeing Patricia again.

Chapter 50

Thomas Sullivan of the Federal Bureau of Investigation had delivered the message to the Forrester family in Tennessee and had to deal with the fall out of the operation. The Forrester women protested going into protective custody but were assured this is what Ben wanted them to do to be safe. They were moved to a small town in upstate New York and changed their name to Bennett. Patricia went to college at the expense of the bureau and eventually became a civil rights activist and moved to Washington DC where she joined an organization that worked with the rights of minorities. She never forgot Joshua Hardgrave and wished she could contact him and let him know she was thinking of him. She wondered what had happened after the dance, the protest about the noose in the tree and whether he ever found his answers about his birth-family. She had always thought their relationship would have developed into more if it hadn't been for the events of the night of the dance.

Joshua was encouraged by his family. His birth and adopted family wanted him to take all the advantages afforded him. He eventually finished his college years at Harvard where he studied law. The events of prom night and the arrest of the local racist groups helped him decide to go into law where he eventually entered into politics. He felt that was where he could do the most good. He could help change laws that affected minorities. He knew that jail was not the place for young black men after hearing the stories from his brother Elisha and Thomas Johnson. He decided his work should make a difference in those areas. He had always been a person with plans and goals, a visionary. After the night of the dance and the reunion with his birth family, he knew the direction he wanted to take. The profession of law would be a good place to start and who knew, he might even run for president one day.

Chapter 51

Rafael and Ramiel met at the kingdoms gates. Rafael said he would go all the way with his friend, but Ramiel said he had to do this on his own. If the Father forgave him, he would be the first to know. Ramiel was before the Father for a long time, prostrating himself with his wings at full spread and his face on the ground. He said he was woefully sorry for his actions. He had allowed himself to be deceived and listened to lies. If he could be forgiven, he would work twice as hard to prove his loyalty. He had helped with Rafael's last assignment and been faithful not to interfere as instructed. His tears wet the marble floor where his face lay. The Father reached forward and took him by the hand and said he had seen his heart. Forgiveness was granted for humans when they asked for it. Today forgiveness was granted for Ramiel because he had come with a pure heart.

Chapter 52

Patricia Bennett had stopped for coffee in a small out of the way coffee house. She was late for a meeting but others were there to cover for her today. There was a sort of melancholy that seemed to surround her. She couldn't put her finger on it. The feelings were reminiscent of times past. Like the incident where the two god-like men rescued her in the alley. Then there was the dream that identified the dark haired stranger rescuing her as a child. She decided he had been her guardian angel. He had been there in her times of need like in the alley. She had begun praying for him. Not to him as much as for him ever since the night she was whisked away to New York. She didn't understand it, but she knew that if she ever needed to be rescued again, she wanted to be sure he was there to help. She took her coffee and went to a table in the back where she could see the door. She had brought some petitions with her and decided while she had a few minutes, she would go over them. It was strange, but she had a sense of a presence near her. She looked around but didn't see anyone, when a well-dressed black man entered through the front door. He had on an expensive pinstriped suit, white shirt and burgundy tie and his shoes were polished shiny black. His hair was close cut and she could tell from her place in the back that he was a professional and extremely handsome. There seemed to be something familiar about him, the way he walked she thought. To her complete surprise, he turned and gave her a broad smile. She immediately recognized him. It was Joshua Hardgrave standing right there five feet from her. She caught her breath and returned his smile. Did he recognize her she wondered or was he just being polite?

Joshua ordered his coffee and paid the barrister? The corner of the condom package he had placed in his wallet years earlier was sticking out. He had carried it as a reminder of that fateful night, the night that changed his life. He smiled to himself, thinking how he never got a chance to use it. He had kept it as a reminder of Patricia Forrester. His father had told him the truth about Patricia's father and he had longed to see her but she had disappeared and he never heard from her again. He headed to the back where she was sitting watching him. He had recognized her immediately when he saw her. She had become a beautiful woman, stylish and still had a perfect body.

"Is this Patricia Forrester before me as I live and breathe?" He said with that smile that melted her heart.

"My name is Patricia Bennett but I do believe we have met before. Would you like to join me? I think we have a lot to catch up on." She moved her papers and signaled for him to take a seat.

"You got married." He said more as a statement than a question since her last name was different, although he didn't see a wedding ring on her finger.

"You are never going to believe what I have to tell you; and no I am not now nor have I ever been married. Actually, I have been waiting for that second kiss you promised me the night of the dance." She blushed but her heart was bursting with excitement. After all this time she still felt the same as she had in high school and she was about to find out if he did too.

Ramiel was stationed at the coffee shop observing the scene below when Rafael arrived. Rafael gave Ramiel a knowing smile and advanced to his side.

"Well here we are Ramiel," Rafael said, "we have come full circle, back to where we were eons before, working together." They stood, stately in appearance and ready to perform their responsibilities with the utmost integrity. Joshua Lance Hardgrave and Patricia Forrester Bennett were to be watched and these angels were to be of assistance throughout their lives

watched

in order for them to fulfill their destinies. Rafael and Ramiel made a good team and they would be faithful until reassigned to a new watch.

The End

Acknowledgments

Many thanks go to Robin Borkholder for editing this work and family and friends who encouraged me to write.